The Wordsworth
Book of Sonnets

The Wordsworth
Book of Sonnets

Edited, with an Introduction,
by Linda Marsh

Wordsworth Poetry Library

This edition published 1995 by Wordsworth Editions Ltd,
Cumberland House, Crib Street, Ware, Hertfordshire SG12 9ET.

ISBN 1-85326-447-4

Typeset in the UK by Antony Gray.
Printed and bound in Denmark by Nørhaven

The paper in this book is produced from pure wood
pulp, without the use of chlorine or any other substance
harmful to the environment. The energy used in its
production consists almost entire of hydroelectricity
and heat generated from waste materials, thereby
converting fossil fuels and contributing little to the
greenhouse effect.

INTRODUCTION

'Personally, I have a dread of the sonnet,' wrote Edward Thomas in a letter. 'It must contain fourteen lines, and a man must be a tremendous poet or a cold mathematician if he can accommodate his thoughts to such a condition.'

'Some Eyes Condemn', his sonnet on page 60, shows how simply and strikingly he used the rhythms of ordinary speech to great effect in what is certainly an exacting verse-form. Its fourteen lines are just long enough for a single theme to be developed, and short enough to test the poet's gift for concentrated expression. Its name is an Italian word for 'little song', and the greatest of sonnets are those in which the poet has overcome the limitations of the form (in the sense that any form imposes strictures), reconciling an adherence to a reasonably rigid set of conventions with his or her own variety and richness of language, tone and mood.

Look at this lovely, pellucid line from Roy Campbell's sonnet, 'The Zebras':

The zebras draw the dawn across the plains . . .

It softly beckons the reader's eye to scan the horizon. You are led to see a movement of colour at the world's edge where the bushveld meets the rising sun, and the loping motion of the animals appears to 'draw' the dawn along. An awesome unity exists between the zebras and the sun; the natural world is working without us, and to our wonder. This is one of the great modern sonnets, and its juxtaposition of such words as 'trampled' and 'lilies' evokes the cruel grandeur of the animal world and the lushness of its flora; its active verbs such as 'roll', 'volted', and 'zithering' indicate the power of the zebra's body. This physicality together with the way the sonnet evokes the smell and colour of the African bush perhaps make it unique. But it shares its form and structure with sonnets written in the fourteenth and fifteenth centuries.

Poets writing sonnets today are drawing on the rich inheritance of the centuries, and what we are seeing in Campbell is not the maturation of a literary form but a contemporary reworking of it. It is exciting to think that the sonnet has survived so long and so potently, retaining its essential features through all the changes in our language and society.

There are two principal kinds of sonnet: the Petrarchan and the Elizabethan. The Petrarchan falls into two divisions. There is a group of eight lines, the octave (rhyming abba abba), followed by a group of six, the sestet (generally rhyming cde cde). The octave usually deals with a situation, an incident or a problem, and the sestet reflects on it and sometimes resolves it. You could say that between the octave and the sestet the sonnet 'turns'; there is some change of direction.

The Shakespearian sonnet is different, consisting of three quatrains (groups of four lines rhyming ab ab cd cd ef ef) and a rhyming couplet (gg). The quatrains state and develop a theme and the couplet clinches the argument or surprises the reader by turning the previous twelve lines on their head. With this pattern, the 'turn' often comes after the twelfth line rather than the eighth.

A fine example of a Petrarchan sonnet can be seen on page 175: Wordsworth's sonnet 'Milton' comprises an octave and a sestet. The octave describes England – its 'stagnant waters' and its moribund people. The sestet describes Milton himself – his virtue and the uniqueness of his presence. His voice, 'whose sound was like the sea' with its freshly breaking waves and rhythmic vibrancy, is in contrast with the stale waters of England's fens. The two sections of the sonnet are linked by such contrasts, and by Wordsworth's own voice, which longingly resonates.

An example of a Shakespearian sonnet can be seen on page 110: 'When I do count the clock . . . ' Its theme is mortality, and the first twelve lines build up a haunting picture of the beauty and shortness of life. These lines are divided up into three quatrains. The first is a reflection on how a day ends. The second concerns the changing seasons of the year – how the trees lose their leaves, with intimations of winter. These thoughts lead Shakespeare to meditate sorrowfully in the third quatrain on the death of his own love's beauty and the shortness of her life. The last two lines introduce a new thought: one way to defeat time is to have children who may carry forward a part of oneself. This thought is expressed in a couplet, the new rhyme reinforcing it.

Milton uses the Petrarchan sonnet form but often omits the octave-sestet pause, so that you could say that there is a third kind of sonnet, the Miltonic. He still retains the rhyme-scheme of the octave and the sestet but holds off the 'turn' and presents it powerfully close to the end. Look at 'On his Blindness' on page 70: one of the great lines in English poetry provides the climax to this sonnet, in which the previous thirteen lines have moved towards these words: 'They also serve who only stand and wait.'

Early Italian sonnets had eleven syllables to each line, and the French used twelve. When the sonnet came to England, the metre adopted was the iambic pentameter. This has ten syllables, every second one of which is stressed. (A basic metrical unit is a foot, which is a combination of stressed and unstressed syllables. When the foot consists of an unstressed followed by a stressed syllable, it is called iambic. The line is named after the number of feet it contains, thus a line having five feet is called a pentameter.) Look again at Campbell's line about the zebra and you can see how this works. It is a miracle of compression: it packs into eight words an event and a symbol; it creates feelings both of movement and stillness, something natural and daily yet also timeless and inspirational, and it moves forward to match the movement and momentum of the animals. Two of the stresses fall on the alliterative 'draw' and 'dawn', and another on 'across', which has the effect of stretching out the plains. A wonder of the world is unfolding rhythmically and continuously. It is a deeply satisfying line, and the zebra's massive force is resolved at the end: 'to roll his mare among the trampled lillies'. The five-foot iambic is perfect for Campbell's purpose; the discipline of the metre charges the action and underpins its meaning.

It was the love poetry of Petrarch that shaped a new course in the writing of verse for the Western European world, and which gave us the first sonnet form that we recognise today. This great Italian poet and scholar, who lived from 1304 to 1374, records that it was in Avignon that he first saw Laura, a burgher's daughter. For the rest of his life he wrote about her beauty and how much she inspired him to love her. There had been poets in Tuscany who had written sonnets with a rudimentary rhyme scheme: Dante, for example, the brilliant and moving writer of *La vita nuova* and the *Divina Commedia,* who lived from 1265 to 1324 and who was himself inspired by a girl he called 'Beatrice'. Even earlier there had been the *corso d'amors* of the troubadours in Provence, the love songs composed by these poet-musicians who had flourished in the 1100s and 1200s in southern France. The tradition of writing verse in praise of physical beauty was well established, and this verse in the Provençal lyric was frequently sensuous and erotic. With time, the ardour of their verses cooled into set responses; a pattern was set by which a poet could praise a lady's loveliness, expect to be rebuffed, and then mourn and worship her by turns. Dante and others deepened this process by seeing the lady not only as lovely in herself but as a symbol representing transcendent beauty and ideal love. What Petrarch brought to these strains of lyric poetry was the powerful combination of a contemplative dimension – in which a real woman lived and was loved, dearly and in a way that gave meaning to the whole of life – and a structure that gave full poetic expression to it. Shifting patterns of rhymes gave way to what is now known as the 'Petrarchan sonnet'.

In England, Sir Philip Sidney held the opinion that between Chaucer and the flowering of the Renaissance there had been no great poetry. In his *Defence of Poetrie* in 1579 he wrote: 'Truly, I know not whether to marvel more, either that he in that misty time could see so clearly, or that we in this clear age walk so stumbling after him.' The period he was so criticising contained much religious poetry, for example in the manuscripts of Simeon, Lambeth and Thornton, some lyric poetry often in ballad metre, and an especially fine volume of carols by Awdlay which Skelton later set to music at the court of Henry VIII. But nothing echoed Chaucer's greatness; and then Sir Thomas Wyatt (1503–42) translated Petrarch's sonnets into English. He experimented with their structure to restyle them with a ten syllabic line and a rhyming couplet. This couplet altered the whole balance of the sestet by ending on a logical note, resolving a tension, clinching an argument or allaying a fear, and thereby affected the whole spirit of the sonnet. Gradually the subject matter changed too, as Wyatt struggled with the process of translating from the Italian, needing to rethink the verbs and the line endings and finding that changes in nuance led to changes in content. Thus the English sonnet was born, but Wyatt died, aged thirty-nine, before pressing on with his experiments to find that if the rhyming of the sestet were to be combined with the rhymes of the preceding two quatrains within the octave, a new unity would be formed. This was discovered by Henry Howard, the Earl of Surrey. Wyatt's and Surrey's work was published in Tottel's famous anthology, *Songes and Sonnettes,* in 1557; and in 1572 Gascoigne's *Sundrie Flowers* appeared, containing thirty-three sonnets; thus other poets were able to see and work with the new form: the Italian roots of Wyatt's early work, and the changes that first he and then Surrey had made.

It was Sir Philip Sidney in the 1580s who took it to new heights with his sonnet sequence *Astrophel and Stella*. This was a collection of one hundred and eight sonnets which proved to be a literary triumph and which led to a craze for sonnet sequences. Astrophel loves Stella passionately, moving towards her with joy and promise, then stepping back in anxiety and conflict. The device of personification enables his complex self to be accompanied by Cupid, who symbolises physical desire, and Love, who represents romance; these two take part in the ups and downs of Astrophel's doomed love affair, and all meet with such figures as Desire, Sense and Reason, who argue for possession or ascendancy. Sidney thus gives Astrophel a very human mixture of tensions in which his infatuation with Stella is at war with his intellectual and spiritual needs, and with the technical control of the sonnet form and Sidney's richness of language a great power was unleashed.

The Elizabethan love sonnet has become justly famous for its light grace and ornate beauty. With Sidney, the great names of Spenser, Drayton and Daniel are among those whose single sonnets and sonnet sequences have enriched the development of the verse-form and broadened its concerns, and with vivid conceits and elegant extravagancies they reflect the intellectual curiosity of the age. John Donne also wrote religious sonnets of an intensely personal kind. As George Herbert wrote in a sonnet addressed to God:

> Doth Poetry
> Wear Venus' livery? Only serve her turn?
> Why are not sonnets made of thee? and layes
> Upon thine altar burnt? Cannot thy love
> Heighten a spirit to sound out thy praise
> As well as any she?

Donne's phrasing and conceits picture the torment he felt inside, moving from the Catholic faith to the Protestant, and from a life in which he had lived freely to one controlled by the claims of the Church. 'Batter my Heart' uses the language of physical love to explain his dilemmas and crises of conscience –

> Except you enthrall me, never shall be free,
> Nor ever chaste, except you ravish me.

– as he searches to find a way of reconciling the violence of his feeling with the exactness of the verse-form. The rhythm and movement of the first four lines hurtle the eye forward as he tries to burst free from God. His passionate and often paradoxical arguments have little of the simplicity shown in 'The Son' where Christ as the son of God and man is also the 'fruitful flame' that lights our world.

The late sixteenth and the early seventeenth centuries produced a ferment of writing in which courtly love, heartfelt desire and spirituality were natural subjects for poets, and eventually Milton wove friendship and the significant events of the day into his own sonnet form with dignity and solemnity. Landor wrote:

> He caught the sonnet from the dainty hand
> of Love, who cried to lose it; and he gave
> The notes to Glory.

But the greatest sonnets that we have are Shakespeare's. In content, form, dramatic texture, richness of language and metaphorical density, his sonnets of love and friendship address truth and mutablity, passion, longing, reciprocity and betrayal and the tyranny of time with unprecedented scope, diversity and power. They are intimately autobiographical, probably not a sequence but a miscellany, and they anticipate, experience and relive every encounter with a beloved that someone living today could imagine. They are written to a young friend and to his mistress, both of whom betray him, and also to a 'rival poet', but Shakespeare has left only slight clues as to their identity, and much debate has centred on who these three really were. Perhaps his friend was the Earl of Southampton; such a relationship certainly freed him to move from the confines of a single Love (the traditional habitat of the poet) into the world of politics and society, thereby stretching the sonnet's concerns to the whole of human life while centring them on this individual. Perhaps the rival was George Chapman – and no one knows who the 'Dark Lady' was, though the speculation is still feverish. But rather as the exact identities of Laura and Beatrice are unknown, it hardly matters. The lyrical intensity of these sonnets is incomparable, endlessly renewing their life and vitality.

Romantic poetry was written during a period of wars and revolutions. Between about 1780 and 1830, brave thinking and writing was going on; such poets as Wordsworth, Coleridge, Keats and Shelley are often thought of as celebrators of rural peace, as escapists, as poets on the edge of history. In fact they were often considered seditious at the time – accused of spying, ostracised for radicalism, one even dying abroad, fighting for Greek independence. Their verse is exciting, and in the ascendancy of the lyric and the narrative, Wordsworth himself wrote more than five hundred sonnets, the best of them amongst the finest there are – see 'Surprised by Joy', for example, on page 90. Keats' 'On First Looking into Chapman's Homer' is considered by many to rank with Shakespeare's highest achievements. He uses the metaphor of voyaging to describe how he discovers the ancient Homer through Chapman's translation; Keats looks with wonder at this work, as Cortez stared silently at the Pacific,

> . . . and all his men
> Look'd at each other with a wild surmise –
> Silent, upon a peak in Darien.

The major English sonnets that were written after the Romantic age were those of Gerard Manley Hopkins (1844–89). In particular, there are six 'sonnets of desolation' or the 'terrible sonnets'. 'If ever anything was written in blood every one of these was,' Hopkins wrote in a letter. Much of the strength of feeling in his work comes from powerful alliteration ('Pitched past pitch of grief . . . ', 'I wake and feel the fell of dark, not day . . . ') and from internal rhyming. It also comes from something entirely new in poetry: he introduced the notion of 'sprung rhythm' to English metre. This involves dispensing with the custom of having a fixed number of syllables in each line, but it does call for a fixed number of strong or stressed syllables per line. There are also 'outriders', which are additionally stressed syllables. While some sonnets are in standard rhythm and of traditional length, others work to this 'sprung rhythm' and are longer ('That Nature is a Hericlitean Fire') or shorter ('Pied Beauty'). He generally preserves the Petrarchan rhyming scheme (abba abba cde cde) and offers his readers this help, should understanding the technicalities of his methods be beyond them! 'Take breath and read it with the ears, as I always wish it to be read, and my verse becomes all right.' This line from 'Spelt from Sibyl's Leaves' shows how inherently musical his verse is:

Our evening is over us; our night whelms, whelms, and will end us.

Another innovator was George Meredith (1828–1909), whose sonnet sequence called *Modern Love* is one of the finest poetical works of the Victorian age, charting the sadness of a marriage slowly disintegrating. Each sonnet is sixteen lines long, those extra two lines extending not only the form but working to draw out the protagonist's sorrow . . . embers instead of a fire burning. Both Hopkins and Meredith proved too idiosyncratic to produce a following, and their sonnet forms have remained distinctly their own.

The first half of the twentieth century saw the sonnet invigorated by war, as the 'soldier poets' firstly sustained a vision of rural England which they must fight to protect – inherited from a long tradition of pastoral elegy, and renewed with the devotional language of 'absolution', 'consecration' and 'sacrifice'. *The Great Sacrifice* was a colour print which the *Graphic* gave away with its Christmas 1914 number, depicting a dying soldier at the foot of the Cross; Rupert Brooke was more than its equal. *Woodbine Willie's Plain Man's Verse* might have been tucked into many pockets in the trenches but Brooke inspired a generation of young men to die for England. With Brooke's own death and the reality of the war revealed in all its cruelty and waste, Wilfred Owen's poetry took the sonnet into a new phase. Its icy control, insightfulness and provocation (which Yeats called 'all blood, dirt and sucked sugar stick') was unlike anything that had been written before.

There are many other great writers of sonnets, and this volume contains only a representative selection, though drawn from all eras of poetry in English from the earliest to the end of the Second World War. It tries to show the longevity of the sonnet form, its richness, its variety, and its impact, and of course I have selected those sonnets which are the loveliest to me. It is awe-inspiring to think that centuries after Petrarch, and miles away in Africa, a poem entitled 'Stroll in Township Twilight' by Themba Hlongwane should be a sonnet:

> Throughout the dusk they stroll along the dark
> and snaky roads segmented by spaced lights . . .

Fourteen lines, three quatrains, and a couplet prove right to describe another world, a moment of violence, a cry of horror. The sonnet is very much alive, and, as Wordsworth wrote,

>   . . . with this key
> Shakespeare unlocked his heart; the melody
> Of this small lute gave ease to Petrarch's wound . . .
> The Sonnet glittered a gay myrtle leaf
> Amid the cypress with which Dante crowned
> His visionary brow: a glow-worm lamp,
> It cheered mild Spenser, called from Faery-land
> To struggle through dark ways . . .

LINDA MARSH

CONTENTS

1   THE WHOLE HEART

2   PARTINGS

3   DESIRE AND PASSION

4   THE PAIN OF LOVE

5   FAITH

6 DESPAIR

7 FAMILY LOVE

10 WAR

11 WRITING

12 DEATH

13   QUESTIONS, DOUBTS, REFLECTIONS

LIST OF AUTHORS

Drummond Allison	1921–44
Matthew Arnold	1822–88
Barnabe Barnes	1569–1609
Thomas Lovell Beddoes	1803–49
Mathilde Blind	1841–96
Wilfrid Scawen Blunt	1840–1922
William Lisle Bowles	1762–1850
H. C. Bradby	1868–1947
Nicholas Breton	1545–1626
Rupert Brooke	1887–1915
Elizabeth Barrett Browning	1806–61
George Gordon Byron	1788 1824
Ada Cambridge	1844–1926
John Clare	1793–1864
Arthur Hugh Clough	1819–61
Hartley Coleridge	1796–1849
Samuel Taylor Coleridge	1772–1834
Henry Constable	1562–1613
William Cowper	1731–1800
Samuel Daniel	1562–1619
John Davies of Hereford	1565–1618
Sir John Davies	1569–1626
John Donne	1572–1631
Lord Alfred Douglas	1870–1945
Michael Drayton	1563–1631
William Drummond	
(of Hawthornden)	1585–1649
George Eliot	1819–80
Sir Richard Fanshawe	1608–66
George Gascoigne	c.1525–77

Thomas Gray	1716–71
Louisa Guggenberger	1845–95
Ivor Gurney	1890–1937
Thomas Hardy	1840–1928
George Herbert	1593–1633
Robert Herrick	1591–1674
May Herschel-Clarke	*dates unknown*
Thomas Hood	1799–1845
Gerald Manley Hopkins	1844–89
Henry Howard, Earl of Surrey	c.1517–47
James Leigh Hunt	1784–1859
Ben Jonson	1572–1637
John Keats	1795–1821
Sidney Keyes	1922–43
King James I	1566–1625
Rudyard Kipling	1865–1936
Emma Lazarus	1849–87
Henry Wadsworth Longfellow	1807–82
John Magee	1922–41
Mary, Queen of Scots	1542–87
Gerald Massey	1828–1907
George Meredith	1828–1909
Alice Meynell	1847–1922
Alice Duer Miller	1874–1942
John Milton	1608–74
Sir Thomas More	1478–1535
William Morris	1834–96
Edith Nesbit	1858–1924
Caroline Norton	1808–77
Wilfred Owen	1893–1918
Sir Walter Ralegh	1552–1618
Lizette Woodworth Reese	1856–35
Edwin Arlington Robinson	1869–1935
Christina Rossetti	1830–94
Dante Gabriel Rossetti	1828–82
William Shakespeare	1564–1616
Percy Bysshe Shelley	1792–1822
Sir Philip Sidney	1554–1586
James Smetham	1821–89
Charles Sorley	1895–1915

Edmund Spenser   *c.*1552–99
Algernon Charles Swinburne   1837–1909
Joshua Sylvester   1563–1618
Alfred, Lord Tennyson   1809–92
Edward Thomas   1878–1917
Charles Tennyson Turner   1808–79
William Walsh   1663–1708
R. E. Egerton Warburton   1804–91
Thomas Warton the Younger   1728–90
Thomas Watson   1557–92
Oscar Wilde   1854–1900
Margaret Willy   *dates unknown*
William Wordsworth   1770–1850
Lady Mary Wroth   *c.*1586–1640
Sir Thomas Wyatt   1503–42
Elinor Wylie   1885–1928
William Butler Yeats   1865–1939

1
THE WHOLE
HEART

The Bargain

My true love hath my heart, and I have his,
  By just exchange, one for the other given.
I hold his dear, and mine he cannot miss,
  There never was a better bargain driven.
His heart in me keeps me and him in one,
  My heart in him his thoughts and senses guides;
He loves my heart, for once it was his own,
  I cherish his, because in me it bides.
His heart his wound receivèd from my sight,
  My heart was wounded with his wounded heart;
For as from me on him his hurt did light,
  So still methought in me his hurt did smart.
    Both equal hurt, in this change sought our bliss:
    My true love hath my heart and I have his.

SIR PHILIP SIDNEY

A Vow to Love Faithfully,
Howsoever He Be Rewarded

Set me whereas the sun doth parch the green
Or where his beams do not dissolve the ice;
In temperate heat, where he is felt and seen;
In presence prest of people, mad or wise;
Set me in high or yet in low degree;
In longest night, or in the shortest day;
In clearest sky, or where clouds thickest be;
In lusty youth, or when my hairs are grey:
Set me in heaven, in earth, or else in hell,
In hill, or dale, or in the foaming flood;
Thrall, or at large, alive whereso I dwell,
Sick, or in health, in evil fame or good,
Hers will I be; and only with this thought
Content myself, although my chance be nought.

HENRY HOWARD, EARL OF SURREY

Were I as base

Were I as base as is the lowly plain
And you, my love, as high as heav'n above,
Yet should the thoughts of me your humble swain
Ascend to heav'n in honour of my love.
Were I as high as heav'n above the plain,
And you, my love, as humble and as low
As are the deepest bottoms of the main,
Wheresoe'er you were, with you my love should go.
Were you the earth, dear love, and I the skies,
My love should shine on you like to the sun,
And look upon you with ten thousand eyes,
Till heav'n waxed blind and till the world were dun.
Wheresoe'er I am, below or else above you,
Wheresoe'er you are, my heart shall truly love you.

JOSHUA SYLVESTER

If chaste and pure devotion

If chaste and pure devotion of my youth
Or glory of my April-springing years,
Unfeignèd love in naked simple truth,
A thousand vows, a thousand sighs and tears;
Or if a world of faithful service done,
Words, thoughts and deeds devoted to her honour,
Or eyes that have beheld her as their sun,
With admiration ever looking on her;
A life that never joyed but in her love,
A soul that ever hath adored her name,
A faith that time nor fortune could not move,
A Muse that unto heaven hath raised her fame:
Though these, nor these, deserve to be embraced,
Yet, fair unkind, too good to be disgraced.

MICHAEL DRAYTON

When men shall find thy flower

When men shall find thy flower, thy glory, pass,
And thou, with careful brow sitting alone,
Receivèd hast this message from thy glass,
That tells the truth and says that all is gone;
Fresh shalt thou see in me the wounds thou madest,
Though spent thy flame, in me the heat remaining:
I that have loved thee thus before thou fadest,
My faith shall wax, when thou art in thy waning.
The world shall find this miracle in me,
That fire can burn when all the matter's spent:
Then what my faith hath been thyself shalt see,
And that thou wast unkind thou may'st repent.
   Thou may'st repent that thou hast scorned my
     tears,
   When winter snows upon thy sable hairs.

SAMUEL DANIEL

Sonnet 109

O, never say that I was false of heart,
Though absence seem'd my flame to qualify.
As easy might I from myself depart
As from my soul, which in thy breast doth lie:
That is my home of love: if I have rangèd,
Like him that travels, l return again;
Just to the time, not with the time exchanged,
So that myself bring water for my stain.
Never believe, though in my nature reign'd
All frailties that besiege all kinds of blood,
That it could so preposterously be stain'd,
To leave for nothing all thy sum of good;
     For nothing this wide universe I call,
     Save thou, my rose; in it thou art my all.

WILLIAM SHAKESPEARE

Sonnet 116

Let me not to the marriage of true minds
Admit impediments. Love is not love
Which alters when it alteration finds,
Or bends with the remover to remove:
O, no! it is an ever-fixèd mark,
That looks on tempests and is never shaken;
It is the star to every wandering bark,
Whose worth's unknown, although his height be taken.
Love's not Time's fool, though rosy lips and cheeks
Within his bending sickle's compass come;
Love alters not with his brief hours and weeks,
But bears it out even to the edge of doom.
　　　If this be error and upon me proved,
　　　　I never writ, nor no man ever loved.

                                    WILLIAM SHAKESPEARE

Sonnet 130

My mistress' eyes are nothing like the sun;
Coral is far more red than her lips' red:
If snow be white, why then her breasts are dun;
If hairs be wires, black wires grow on her head.
I have seen roses damask'd, red and white,
But no such roses see I in her cheeks;
And in some perfumes is there more delight
Than in the breath that from my mistress reeks.
I love to hear her speak, yet well I know
That music hath a far more pleasing sound:
I grant I never saw a goddess go,
My mistress, when she walks, treads on the ground:
　　　And yet, by heaven, I think my love as rare
　　　　As any she belied with false compare.

                                    WILLIAM SHAKESPEARE

Sonnet written on a blank page in Shakespeare's Poems

Bright star! would I were stedfast as thou art –
   Not in lone splendour hung aloft the night
And watching, with eternal lids apart,
   Like Nature's patient, sleepless Eremite,
The moving waters at their priestlike task
   Of pure ablution round earth's human shores,
Or gazing on the new soft fallen mask
   Of snow upon the mountains and the moors –
No – yet still stedfast, still unchangeable,
   Pillow'd upon my fair love's ripening breast,
To feel for ever its soft fall and swell,
   Awake for ever in a sweet unrest,
Still, still to hear her tender-taken breath,
And so live ever – or else swoon to death.

JOHN KEATS

Now sleeps the crimson petal

Now sleeps the crimson petal, now the white;
Nor waves the cypress in the palace walk;
Nor winks the gold fin in the porphyry font:
The fire-fly wakens: waken thou with me.

Now droops the milkwhite peacock like a ghost,
And like a ghost she glimmers on to me.

Now lies the earth all Danaë to the stars,
And all thy heart lies open unto me.

Now slides the silent meteor on, and leaves
A shining furrow, as thy thoughts in me.

Now folds the lily all her sweetness up,
And slips into the bosom of the lake:
So fold thyself, my dearest, thou, and slip
Into my bosom and be lost in me.

ALFRED TENNYSON

If thou must love me

If thou must love me, let it be for nought
Except for love's sake only. Do not say
'I love her for her smile . . . her look . . . her way
Of speaking gently, . . . for a trick of thought
That falls in well with mine, and certes brought
A sense of pleasant ease on such a day' –
For these things in themselves, Beloved, may
Be changed, or change for thee, – and love, so wrought,
May be unwrought so. Neither love me for
Thine own dear pity's wiping my cheeks dry, –
A creature might forget to weep, who bore
Thy comfort long, and lose thy love thereby!
But love me for love's sake, that evermore
Thou mayst love on, through love's eternity.

ELIZABETH BARRETT BROWNING

When our two souls

When our two souls stand up erect and strong,
Face to face, silent, drawing nigh and nigher,
Until the lengthening wings break into fire
At either curvèd point, – what bitter wrong
Can the earth do to us, that we should not long
Be here contented? Think. In mounting higher,
The angels would press on us and aspire
To drop some golden orb of perfect song
Into our deep, dear silence. Let us stay
Rather on earth, Belovèd, – where the unfit
Contrarious moods of men recoil away
And isolate pure spirits, and permit
A place to stand and love in for a day,
With darkness and the death-hour rounding it.

ELIZABETH BARRETT BROWNING

First time he kissed me

First time he kissed me, he but only kissed
The fingers of this hand wherewith I write;
And ever since, it grew more clean and white,
Slow to world-greetings, quick with its 'Oh, list,'
When the angels speak. A ring of amethyst
I could not wear here, plainer to my sight,
Than that first kiss. The second passed in height
The first, and sought the forehead, and half missed,
Half falling on the hair. O beyond meed!
That was the chrism of love, which love's own crown,
With sanctifying sweetness, did precede.
The third upon my lips was folded down
In perfect, purple state; since when, indeed,
I have been proud and said, 'My love, my own.'

ELIZABETH BARRETT BROWNING

How do I love thee?

How do I love thee? Let me count the ways,
I love thee to the depth and breadth and height
My soul can reach, when feeling out of sight
For the ends of Being and ideal Grace.

I love thee to the level of everyday's
Most quiet need, by sun and candlelight.
I love thee freely, as men strive for Right;
I love thee purely, as they turn from Praise.

I love thee with the passion put to use
In my old griefs, and with my childhood's faith.
I love thee with a love I seemed to lose

With my lost saints – I love thee with the breath,
Smiles, tears, of all my life! – and, if God choose
I shall but love thee better after death.

ELIZABETH BARRETT BROWNING

How do I Love Thee?

I cannot woo thee as the lion his mate,
With proud parade and fierce prestige of presence;
Nor thy fleet fancy may I captivate
With pastoral attitudes in flowery pleasance;
Nor will I kneeling court thee with sedate
And comfortable plans of husbandhood;
Nor file before thee as a candidate . . .
I cannot woo thee as a lover would.

To wrest thy hand from rivals, iron-gloved,
Or cheat them by a craft, I am not clever.
But I do love thee even as Shakespeare loved,
Most gently wild, and desperately for ever,
Full-hearted, grave, and manfully in vain,
With thought, high pain, and ever vaster pain.

WILFRED OWEN

My shy hand

My shy hand shades a hermitage apart, —
　　O large enough for thee, and thy brief hours.
Life there is sweeter held than in God's heart,
　　Stiller than in the heavens of hollow flowers.

The wine is gladder there than in gold bowls.
　　And Time shall not drain thence, nor trouble spill.
Sources between my fingers feed all souls,
　　Where thou mayest cool thy lips, and draw thy fill.

Five cushions hath my hand, for reveries;
　　And one deep pillow for thy brow's fatigues;
Languor of June all winterlong, and ease
　　For ever from the vain untravelled leagues.

Thither your years may gather in from storm,
And Love, that sleepeth there, will keep thee warm.

WILFRED OWEN

2

PARTINGS

Finding those beames, which I must ever love

Finding those beames, which I must ever love,
  To marre my minde, and with my hurt to please,
I deemd it best some absence for to prove,
  If further place might further me to ease.

Myne eyes thence drawne, where lived all their light,
  Blinded forthwith in darke dispaire did lye,
Like to the Mowlle with want of guiding sight,
  Deepe plunged in earth, deprivèd of the skie.

In absence blind, and wearied with that woe,
  To greater woes by presence I returne,
Even as the flye, which to the name doth goe,
  Pleased with the light, that his small corse doth burne:
    Faire choice I have, either to live or dye
    A blinded Mowlle, or else a burnèd flye.

SIR PHILIP SIDNEY

A Farewell

Oft have I mused, but now at length I find,
Why those that die, men say they do depart.
'Depart!' – a word so gentle, to my mind,
Weakly did seem to paint death's ugly dart.
But now the stars, with their strange course, do bind
Me one to leave, with whom I leave my heart;
I hear a cry of spirits, faint and blind,
That, parting thus, my chiefest part I part.
Part of my life, the loathèd part to me,
Lives to impart my weary clay some breath;
But that good part, wherein all comforts be,
Now dead, doth show departure is a death –

Yea, worse than death: death parts both woe and joy:
From joy I part, still living in annoy.

SIR PHILIP SIDNEY

Since there's no help

Since there's no help, come let us kiss and part:
Nay, I have done; you get no more of me;
And I am glad, yea, glad with all my heart
That thus so cleanly I myself can free.
Shake hands forever; cancel all our vows;
And when we meet at any time again,
Be it not seen in either of our brows
That we one jot of former love retain.
Now at the last gasp of love's latest breath
When, his pulse failing, passion speechless lies,
When faith is kneeling by his bed of death
And innocence is closing up his eyes;
    Now, if thou would'st, when all have given him over,
    From Death to Life thou might'st him yet recover.

MICHAEL DRAYTON

Sonnet 87

Farewell! thou art too dear for my possessing,
And like enough thou know'st thy estimate:
The charter of thy worth gives thee releasing;
My bonds in thee are all determinate.
For how do I hold thee but by thy granting?
And for that riches where is my deserving?
The cause of this fair gift in me is wanting,
And so my patent back again is swerving.
Thyself thou gavest, thy own worth then not knowing,
Or me, to whom thou gavest it, else mistaking;
So thy great gift, upon misprision growing,
Comes home again, on better judgement making.
    Thus have I had thee, as a dream doth flatter,
    In sleep a king, but waking no such matter.

WILLIAM SHAKESPEARE

At Dover Cliffs, July 20, 1787

On these white cliffs, that calm above the flood
Uplift their shadowing heads, and, at their feet,
Scarce hear the surge that has for ages beat,
Sure many a lonely wanderer has stood;
And, whilst the lifted murmur met his ear,
And o'er the distant billows the still Eve
Sailed slow, has thought of all his heart must leave
Tomorrow; of the friends he loved most dear;
Of social scenes, from which he wept to part;
But if, like me, he knew how fruitless all
The thoughts that would full fain the past recall,
Soon would he quell the risings of his heart,
And brave the wild winds and unhearing tide,
The world his country, and his God his guide.

WILLIAM LISLE BOWLES

Renouncement

I must not think of thee; and, tired yet strong,
  I shun the thought that lurks in all delight –
    The thought of thee – and in the blue Heaven's height,
And in the sweetest passage of a song.
O just beyond the fairest thoughts that throng
  This breast, the thought of thee waits hidden yet bright;
    But it must never, never come in sight;
I must stop short of thee the whole day long.
But when sleep comes to close each difficult day,
  When night gives pause to the long watch I keep
    And all my bonds I needs must loose apart,
Must doff my will as raiment laid away, –
  With the first dream that comes with the first sleep
    I run, I run, I am gathered to thy heart.

ALICE MEYNELL

Many in after times will say of you

Many in after times will say of you
'He loved her' – while of me what will they say?
Not that I loved you more than just in play,
For fashion's sake as idle women do.
Even let them prate; who know not what we knew
Of love and parting in exceeding pain,
Of parting hopeless here to meet again,
Hopeless on earth, and heaven is out of view.
But by my heart of love laid bare to you,
My love that you can make not void nor vain,
Love that foregoes you but to claim anew
Beyond this passage of the gate of death,
I charge you at the Judgment make it plain
My love of you was life and not a breath.

CHRISTINA ROSSETTI

If there be any one

Amor che ne la mente mi ragiona – DANTE
Amor vien nel bel viso di costei – PETRARCA

If there be any one can take my place
   And make you happy whom I grieve to grieve,
   Think not that I can grudge it, but believe
I do commend you to that nobler grace,
That readier wit than mine, that sweeter face;
   Yea, since your riches make me rich, conceive
   I too am crowned, while bridal crowns I weave,
And thread the bridal dance with jocund pace.
For if I did not love you, it might be
   That I should grudge you some one dear delight;
     But since the heart is yours that was mine own,
   Your pleasure is my pleasure, right my right,
Your honourable freedom makes me free,
     And you companioned I am not alone.

CHRISTINA ROSSETTI

Go from me

Go from me. Yet I feel that I shall stand
Henceforward in thy shadow. Nevermore
Alone upon the threshold of my door
Of individual life, I shall command

The uses of my soul, nor lift my hand
Serenely in the sunshine as before,
Without the sense of that which I forbore, . .
Thy touch upon the palm. The widest land

Doom takes to part us, leaves thy heart in mine
With pulses that beat double. What I do
And what I dream includes thee, as the wine

Must taste of its own grapes. And when I sue
God for myself, He hears that name of thine,
And sees within my eyes, the tears of two.

                          ELIZABETH BARRETT BROWNING

The Mute Lovers on the Railway Journey

They bade farewell; but neither spoke of love.
The railway bore him off with rapid pace,
He gazed awhile on Edith's garden grove,
Till alien woodlands overlapp'd the place –
Alas! he cried, how mutely did we part!
I fear'd to test the truth I seem'd to see.
Oh! that the love dream in her timid heart
Had sigh'd itself awake, and called for me!
I could have answer'd with a ready mouth,
And told a sweeter dream; but each forebore.
He saw the hedgerows fleeting to the north
On either side, whilst he look'd sadly forth:
Then set himself to face the vacant south,
While fields and woods ran back to Edith More.

                          CHARLES TENNYSON TURNER

Be frank with me

Be frank with me, and I accept my lot;
    But deal not with me as a grieving child,
Who for the loss of that which he hath not
    Is by a show of kindness thus beguiled.
Raise not for me, from its enshrouded tomb,
    The ghostly likeness of a hope deceased;
Nor think to cheat the darkness of my doom
    By wavering doubts how far thou art released:
This dressing pity in the garb of Love,
    This effort of the heart to *seem* the same, –
These sighs and lingerings, (which nothing prove
    But that thou leavest me with a kind of shame,) –
Remind me more, by their most vain deceit,
Of the dear loss of all which thou dost counterfeit.

CAROLINE NORTON

Am I to lose you?

'Am I to lose you now?' The words were light;
    You spoke them, hardly seeking a reply,
    That day I bid you quietly 'Good-bye,'
And sought to hide my soul away from sight.
The question echoed, dear, through many a night, –
    My question, not your own – most wistfully;
'Am I to lose him?' – asked my heart of me;
'Am I to lose him now, and lose him quite?'

And only you can tell me. Do you care
    That sometimes we in quietness should stand
    As fellow-solitudes, hand firm in hand,
And thought with thought and hope with hope compare?
What is your answer? Mine must ever be,
    'I greatly need your friendship: leave it me.'

LOUISA GUGGENBERGER

The Busy Heart

Now that we've done our best and worst, and parted,
  I would fill my mind with thoughts that will not rend
(O heart, I do not dare go empty-hearted)
  I'll think of Love in books, Love without end;
Women with child, content; and old men sleeping;
  And wet strong ploughlands, scarred for certain grain;
And babes that weep, and so forget their weeping;
  And the young heavens, forgetful after rain;
And evening hush, broken by homing wings;
  And Song's nobility, and Wisdom holy,
That live, we dead. I would think of a thousand things,
  Lovely and durable, and taste them slowly,
One after one, like tasting a sweet food.
I have need to busy my heart with quietude.

                                        RUPERT BROOKE

He Wonders Whether to
Praise or to Blame Her

I have peace to weigh your worth, now all is over,
    But if to praise or blame you, cannot say.
For, who decries the loved, decries the lover;
    Yet what man lauds the thing he's thrown away?

Be you, in truth, this dull, slight, cloudy naught,
    The more fool I, so great a fool to adore;
But if you're that high goddess once I thought,
    The more your godhead is, I lose the more.

Dear fool, pity the fool who thought you clever!
    Dear wisdom, do not mock the fool that missed you!
Most fair, – the blind has lost your face for ever!
    Most foul, – how could I see you while I kissed you?

So . . . the poor love of fools and blind I've proved you,
For, foul or lovely, 'twas a fool that loved you.

                                        RUPERT BROOKE

The Kestrels

When I would think of you, my mind holds only
The small defiant kestrels – how they cut
The raincloud with sharp wings, continually circling
About a storm-rocked elm, with passionate cries.
It was an early month. The plow cut hard.
The may was knobbed with chilly buds. My folly
Was great enough to lull away my pride.

There is no virtue now in blind reliance
On place or person or the forms of love.
The storm bears down the pivotal tree, the cloud
Turns to the net of an inhuman fowler
And drags us from the air. Our wings are clipped.
Yet still our love and luck lies in our parting:
Those cries and wings surprise our surest act.

                                        SIDNEY KEYES

3

DESIRE AND
PASSION

Like as a huntsman after weary chase

Like as a huntsman after weary chase,
Seeing the game from him escaped away,
Sits down to rest him in some shady place,
With panting hounds beguilèd of their prey:
So after long pursuit and vain assay,
When I all weary had the chase forsook,
The gentle deer returned the self-same way,
Thinking to quench her thirst at the next brook.
There she beholding me with milder look,
Sought not to fly, but fearless still did bide:
Till I in hand her yet half trembling took,
And with her own goodwill her firmly tied.
 Strange thing me seemed to see a beast so wild,
 So goodly won with her own will beguiled.

EDMUND SPENSER

Fair bosom

Fair bosom fraught with virtue's richest treasure,
 The nest of love, the lodging of delight:
 The bower of bliss, the paradise of pleasure,
 The sacred harbour of that heavenly sprite.
How was I ravished with your lovely sight,
 And my frail thoughts too rashly led astray?
 Whiles diving deep through amorous insight,
 On the sweet spoil of beauty they did prey.
And twixt her paps like early fruit in May,
 Whose harvest seemed to hasten now apace:
 They loosely did their wanton wings display,
 And there to rest themselves did boldly place.
Sweet thoughts I envy your so happy rest,
 Which oft I wished, yet never was so blessed.

EDMUND SPENSER

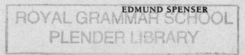

Coming to kiss her lips

Coming to kiss her lips, (such grace I found)
　　Me seemed I smelt a garden of sweet flowers:
　　That dainty odours from them threw around
　　For damsels fit to deck their lovers' bowers.
Her lips did smell like unto gillyflowers,
　　Her ruddy cheeks like unto roses red: |
　　Her snowy brows like budded bellamoures,
　　Her lovely eyes like pinks but newly spread.
Her goodly bosom like a strawberry bed,
　　Her neck like to a bunch of colombines:
　　Her breast like lillies, ere their leaves be shed,
　　Her nipples like young blossomed jessamines.
Such fragrant flowers do give most odorous smell,
　　But her sweet odour did them all excell.

                                        EDMUND SPENSER

I saw the object of my pining thought

I saw the object of my pining thought
Within a garden of sweet Nature's placing;
Wherein an arbour, artificial wrought,
By workman's wondrous skill the garden gracing,
Did boast his glory, glory far renownèd,
For in his shady boughs my mistress slept:
And with a garland of his branches crownèd,
Her dainty forehead from the sun ykept.
Imperious Love upon her eyelids tending,
Playing his wanton sports at every beck,
And into every finest limb descending,
From eyes to lips, from lips to ivory neck;
　　And every limb supplied, and t' every part
　　Had free ac'cess, but durst not touch her heart.

                                        THOMAS WATSON

Thou blind man's mark . . .

Thou blind man's mark, thou fool's self-chosen snare,
Fond Fancy's scum and dregs of scattered thought,
Band of all evils, cradle of causeless care,
Thou web of will whose end is never wrought:
Desire! desire, I have too dearly bought
With price of mangled mind thy worthless ware;
Too long, too long asleep thou hast me brought,
Who should my mind to higher things prepare.
But yet in vain thou hast my ruin sought,
In vain thou mad'st me to vain things aspire,
In vain thou kindlest all thy smoky fire.
For virtue hath this better lesson taught,
Within myself to seek my only hire,
Desiring nought but how to kill desire.

                                        SIR PHILIP SIDNEY

To Anthea

Ah my Anthea! must my heart still break?
(*Love makes me write, what shame forbids to speak.*)
Give me a kiss, and to that kiss a score;
Then to that twenty, add an hundred more:
A thousand to that hundred: so kiss on,
To make that thousand up a million.
Treble that million, and when that is done,
Let's kiss afresh, as when we first begun.
But yet, though love likes well such scenes as these,
There is an act that will more fully please:
Kissing and glancing, soothing, all make way
But to the acting of this private play:
Name it I would; but being blushing red,
The rest I'll speak, when we meet both in bed.

                                        ROBERT HERRICK

The Author loving these homely meats specially,
viz.: cream, pancakes, buttered pippin-pies
(laugh, good people) and tobacco; writ to that worthy and
virtuous gentlewoman, whom he calleth mistress, as followeth

If there were, oh! an Hellespont of cream
Between us, milk-white mistress, I would swim
To you, to show to both my love's extreme,
Leander-like, – yea! dive from brim to brim.
But met I with a buttered pippin-pie
Floating upon't, that would I make my boat
To waft me to you without jeopardy,
Though sea-sick I might be while it did float.
Yet if a storm should rise, by night or day,
Of sugar-snows and hail of caraways,
Then, if I found a pancake in my way,
It like a plank should bring me to your kays;
    Which having found, if they tobacco kept,
    The smoke should dry me well before I slept.

JOHN DAVIES OF HEREFORD

Sonnet 57

Being your slave, what should I do but tend
Upon the hours and times of your desire?
I have no precious time at all to spend,
Nor services to do, till you require.
Nor dare I chide the world-without-end hour
Whilst I, my sovereign, watch the clock for you,
Nor think the bitterness of absence sour
When you have bid your servant once adieu;
Nor dare I question with my jealous thought
Where you may be, or your affairs suppose,
But, like a sad slave, stay and think of nought
Save, where you are how happy you make those.
 So true a fool is love that in your will,
 Though you do any thing, he thinks no ill.

WILLIAM SHAKESPEARE

If I profane

ROMEO   (*Taking* JULIET'S *hand*)

If I profane with my unworthiest hand
This holy shrine, the gentle sin is this:
My lips, two blushing pilgrims, ready stand
To smooth that rough touch with a tender kiss.

JULIET   Good pilgrim, you do wrong your hand too much,
Which mannerly devotion shows in this;
For saints have hands that pilgrims' hands do touch,
And palm to palm is holy palmers' kiss.

ROMEO   Have not saints lips, and holy palmers too?

JULIET   Ay, pilgrim, lips that they must use in prayer.

ROMEO   O then, dear saint, let lips do what hands do:
They pray, 'Grant thou, lest faith turn to despair.'

JULIET   Saints do not move, though grant for prayers' sake.

ROMEO   Then move not, while my prayer's effect I take.

He kisses her.

WILLIAM SHAKESPEARE

Chorus from Romeo and Juliet, Act 2

Now old Desire doth in his death-bed lie,
    And young Affection gapes to be his heir;
That fair for which love groaned for and would die,
    With tender Juliet matched, is now not fair.
Now Romeo is beloved and loves again,
    Alike bewitchèd by the charm of looks,
But to his foe-supposed he must complain,
    And she steal love's sweet bait from fearful hooks:
Being held a foe, he may not have access
    To breathe such vows as lovers use to swear;
And she as much in love, her means much less
    To meet her new-belovèd anywhere;
But passion lends them power, time means, to meet,
    Tempering extremities with extreme sweet.

                                  WILLIAM SHAKESPEARE

To Fanny

I cry your mercy – pity – love! – ay, love!
    Merciful love that tantalises not
One-thoughted, never-wandering, guileless love,
    Unmask'd, and being seen – without a blot!
O! let me have thee whole, – all – all – be mine!
    That shape, that fairness, that sweet minor zest
Of love, your kiss, – those hands, those eyes divine,
    That warm, white, lucent, million-pleasured breast,
Yourself – your soul – in pity give me all,
    Withhold no atom's atom or I die,
Or living on, perhaps, your wretched thrall,
    Forget, in the mist of idle misery,
Life's purposes, – the palate of my mind
Losing its gust, and my ambition blind!

                                    JOHN KEATS

Nuptial Sleep

At length their long kiss severed, with sweet smart:
  And as the last slow sudden drops are shed
  From sparkling eaves when all the storm has fled,
So singly flagged the pulses of each heart.
Their bosoms sundered, with the opening start
  Of married flowers to either side outspread
  From the knit stem; yet still their mouths, burnt red,
Fawned on each other where they lay apart.

Sleep sank them lower than the tide of dreams,
  And their dreams watched them sink, and slid away.
Slowly their souls swam up again, through gleams
  Of watered light and dull drowned waifs of day;
Till from some wonder of new woods and streams
  He woke, and wondered more: for there she lay.

                                    DANTE GABRIEL ROSSETTI

The Kiss

What smouldering senses in death's sick delay
  Or seizure of malign vicissitude
  Can rob this body of honour, or denude
This soul of wedding-raiment worn today?
For lo! even now my lady's lips did play
  With these my lips such consonant interlude
  As laurelled Orpheus longed for when he wooed
The half-drawn hungering face with that last lay.

I was a child beneath her touch, – a man
When breast to breast we clung, even I and she –
  A spirit when her spirit looked through me –
A god when all our life-breath met to fan
Our life-blood, till love's emulous ardours ran,
  Fire within fire, desire in deity.

                                    DANTE GABRIEL ROSSETTI

Love and Sleep

Lying asleep between the strokes of night
   I saw my love lean over my sad bed,
   Pale as the duskiest lily's leaf or head,
Smooth-skinned and dark, with bare throat made to bite,
Too wan for blushing and too warm for white,
   But perfect-coloured without white or red.
   And her lips opened amorously, and said –
I wist not what, saving one word – Delight.

And all her face was honey to my mouth,
   And all her body pasture to mine eyes;
     The long lithe arms and hotter hands than fire,
The quivering flanks, hair smelling of the south,
   The bright light feet, the splendid supple thighs
     And glittering eyelids of my soul's desire.

ALGERNON CHARLES SWINBURNE

False Prophet

When I was forty, and two feathers sprung
Like crescents silver-curved from either temple,
Above a casque of bronze, I saw the simple
And casual shape of beauty; and my tongue
Spoke thus: 'I am rejoiced I am not young
Lest this supreme and ultimate example
Of fine-spun flesh should very lightly trample
Upon my wounds; my withers are unwrung.'

He might have been my son, save that my youth,
Bending the slender bow of its despair,
Loosed no such luminous arrow on the air;
His shaft was cut from some diviner bough:
And while my fainting heart perceived the truth,
My tongue spoke thus: 'He cannot hurt me now.'

ELINOR WYLIE

The Sleeping Beauty

Sojourning through a southern realm in youth,
I came upon a house by happy chance
Where bode a marvellous Beauty. There, romance
Flew faerily until I lit on truth –
For lo! the fair Child slumbered. Though, forsooth,
She lay not blanketed in drowsy trance,
But leapt alert of limb and keen of glance,
From sun to shower; from gaiety to ruth;
Yet breathed her loveliness asleep in her:
For, when I kissed, her eyelids knew no stir.
So back I drew tiptoe from that Princess,
Because it was too soon, and not my part,
To start voluptuous pulses in her heart,
And kiss her to the world of Consciousness.

WILFRED OWEN

A Memory

Somewhile before the dawn I rose, and stept
   Softly along the dim way to your room,
   And found you sleeping in the quiet gloom,
And holiness about you as you slept.
I knelt there; till your waking fingers crept
   About my head, and held it. I had rest
   Unhoped this side of Heaven, beneath your breast.
I knelt a long time, still; nor even wept.

It was great wrong you did me; and for gain
Of that poor moment's kindliness, and ease,
And sleepy mother-comfort!
                Child, you know
How easily love leaps out to dreams like these,
Who has seen them true. And love that's wakened so
Takes all too long to lay asleep again.

RUPERT BROOKE

Leda and the Swan

A sudden blow: the great wings beating still
Above the staggering girl, her thighs caressed
By the dark webs, her nape caught in his bill,
He holds her helpless breast upon his breast.

How can those terrified vague fingers push
The feathered glory from her loosening thighs?
And how can body, laid in that white rush,
But feel the strange heart beating where it lies?

A shudder in the loins engenders there
The broken wall, the burning roof and tower
And Agamemnon dead.
                     Being so caught up,
So mastered by the brute blood of the air,
Did she put on his knowledge with his power
Before the indifferent beak could let her drop?

WILLIAM BUTLER YEATS

4

THE PAIN
OF LOVE

Rime 134

I fynde no peace and all my warr is done;
    I fere and hope I burne and freise like yse;
    I fley above the wynde yet can I not arrise;
    And noght I have and all the worold I seson.
That loseth nor locketh holdeth me in prison
    And holdeth me not, yet can I scape no wise;
    Nor letteth me Iyve nor dye at my devise,
    And yet of deth it gyveth me occasion.
Withoute Iyen, I se; and withoute tong I plain;
    I desire to perisshe and yet I aske helthe;
    I love an othre and thus I hate my self;
I fede me in sorrowe and laugh in all my pain;
    Likewise displeaseth me boeth deth and lyffe;
    And my delite is causer of this stryff.

SIR THOMAS WYATT

Rime 190

From the Italian of Petrarch

Who so list to hounte I know where is an hynde;
    But as for me, helas, I may no more:
    The vayne travaill hath weried me so sore,
    I ame of theim that farthest cometh behinde;
Yet may I by no meanes my weried mynde
    Drawe from the Diere: but as she fleeth afore
    Faynting I folowe; I leve of therefore,
    Sithens in a nett I seke to hold the wynde.
Who list her hount I put him owte of dowbte,
    As well as I may spend his tyme in vain:
    And graven with Diamondes in letters plain
There is written her faier neck rounde abowte:
    'Noli me tangere for Cesars I ame,
    And wylde for to hold though I seme tame'.

SIR THOMAS WYATT

Uppon the Devyse of a Seeled Dove, with this worde of Petrarch:
Non mi vuol e non mi trahe d'Impaccio

Like as the Dove which seeled up doth flie,
   Is neither freed, nor yet to service bound,
But hopes to gaine some helpe by mounting hie,
   Till want of force do force her fall to ground;

Right so my minde, caught by his guiding eye
   And thence cast off, where his sweete hurt he found,
Hath neither leave to live, nor doome to dye,
   Nor held in evill, nor suffered to be sound,

But with his wings of fancies up he goes,
   To hie conceits whose fruits are oft but small,
Till wounded, blind, and wearied Spirites, lose
   Both force to flie and knowledge where to fall.
      O happie Dove if she no bondage tried:
      More happie I, might I in bondage bide.

SIR PHILIP SIDNEY

With how sad steps, ô Moone, thou climb'st the skies

With how sad steps, ô Moone, thou climb'st the skies,
How silently, and with how wanne a face,
What, may it be that even in heav'nly place
That busie archer his sharpe arrowes tries?
Sure, if that long with *Love* acquainted eyes
Can judge of *Love*, thou feel'st a Lover's case;
I reade it in thy lookes, thy languisht grace,
To me that feele the like, thy state descries.
Then ev'n of fellowship, ô Moone, tell me
Is constant *Love* deem'd there but want of wit?
Are Beauties there as proud as here they be?
Do they above love to be lov'd, and yet
Those Lovers scorne whom that *Love* doth possesse?
Do they call *Vertue* there ungratefulnesse?

SIR PHILIP SIDNEY

Rime 140

From the Italian of Petrarch

Love that doth raine and live within my thought,
and buylt his seat within my captyve brest,
Clad in the armes wherein with me he fowght,
Oft in my face he doth his banner rest.
But she that tawght me love and suffre paine,
My doubtful hope and eke my hote desire
With shamfast looke to shadoo and refrayne,
Her smyling grace convertyth streight to yre.
And cowarde Love, then, to the hart apace
Taketh his flight, where he doth lurke and playne
His purpose lost, and dare not shew his face.
For my lordes gilt thus fawtles byde I payine;
Yet from my lorde shall not my foote remove:
Sweet is the death that taketh end by love.

                              HENRY HOWARD, EARL OF SURREY

Late in the Forest

Late in the Forest I did Cupid see
  Colde, wett, and crying hee had lost his way,
  And beeing blind was farder like to stray:
  Which sight a kind compassion bred in mee,

I kindly tooke, and dride him, while that hee
  Poore child complain'd hee stervèd was with stay,
  And pin'de for want of his accustom'd pray,
  For non in that wilde place his hoste would bee,

I glad was of his finding, thinking sure
  This service should my freedome still procure,
  And in my armes I tooke him then unharmde,

Carrying him safe unto a Mirtle bowre
  Butt in the way hee made mee feele his powre,
  Burning my heart who had him kindly warmd.

LADY MARY WROTH

You blessed shades

You blessed shades, which give mee silent rest,
    Wittnes butt this when death hath clos'd mine eyes,
    And separated mee from earthly ties,
    Beeing from hence to higher place adrest;

How oft in you I have laine heere oprest,
    And have my miseries in woefull cries
    Deliver'd forth, mounting up to the skies
    Yett helples back returnd to wound my brest,

Which wounds did butt strive how, to breed more harme
    To mee, who can bee cur'de by noe one charme
    Butt that of love, which yett may mee releeve;

If nott, lett death my former paines redeeme,
    My trusty freinds, my faith untouch'd esteeme
    And wittnes I could love, who soe could greeve.

                                   LADY MARY WROTH

Lacking my Love

Lacking my Love, I go from place to place,
Like a young fawn that late hath lost the hind,
And seek each where, where last I saw her face,
Whose image yet I carry fresh in mind.
I seek the fields with her late footing signed;
I seek her bower with her late presence decked;
Yet nor in field nor bower I her can find;
Yet field and bower are full of her as'pect:
But when mine eyes I thereunto direct,
They idly back return to me again:
And when I hope to see their true ob'ject,
I find my self but fed with fancies vain.
    Cease then, mine eyes, to seek her self to see;
    And let my thoughts behold her self in me.

EDMUND SPENSER

For that he looked not upon her

You must not wonder, though you think it strange,
To see me hold my louring head so low;
And that mine eyes take no delight to range
About the gleams which on your face do grow.
The mouse which once hath broken out of trap,
Is seldom 'ticèd with the trustless bait,
But lies aloof for fear of more mishap,
And feedeth still in doubt of deep deceit.
The scorchèd fly, which once hath 'scaped the flame,
Will hardly come to play again with fire:
Whereby I learn that grievous is the game
Which follows fancy dazzled by desire:
    So that I wink or else hold down my head,
    Because your blazing eyes my bale have bred.

GEORGE GASCOIGNE

Sonnet 6

Into his hands, utterly into his power,
   I place my son, my life, my honour and all
My Subjects and my country, being in thrall
To him so fast that daily, hour by hour,
My all-surrendered soul hath no intent
   But, despite any trouble which may ensue,
   To make him see that my great love is true,
And that my constancy is permanent.

   Storm or fair weather, let come what come may!
   My soul has found its bourne and there shall stay.
Soon will I give him proof beyond all fears
   That I am one faithful with no disguise,
And not by feign'd submission or false tears,
   As others use, but in quite different wise.

MARY STUART, QUEEN OF SCOTS

Sonnet 7

When you so wildly loved her, she was cold;
   And when your suffering brought you near to madness,
As comes to all whose love is uncontrolled,
   She did but counterfeit a little sadness
That – she could catch no joy from your fierce fire.
   Her dresses proved that in her own proud view
No imperfections, howsoever dire,
   Could blot her image from a heart so true.
I saw in her no right and proper dread
   Lest such a husband, such a man, should die.
You gave her all she is; and she, instead
   Of glorying in the hour that sealed your fate,*
   Has never prized it at its own just rate:
Yet you can say you loved her desperately!

MARY STUART, QUEEN OF SCOTS

* probably refers to Bothwells's wedding day

Sonnet 8

That you trust *her*, alas, is plain enough
   And that you doubt *my* truth is all too plain.
O my Sole Wealth and my One Only Love,
   I strive to make you sure of me – in vain:
You think me light, as far too well I see,
   And watch me with suspicion all day long
Though without cause: whereby you do to me,
Dear Heart, a very great and grievous wrong.
You little know what love to you I bear;
   You even fear lest someone else may win me;
You look upon my words as empty air,
   And think my heart is weak as wax within me;
You count me a vain woman without sense:
Yet all you do makes my love more intense.

MARY STUART, QUEEN OF SCOTS

Sonnet 10

I seek but one thing – to make sure of You
   Who are the sole sustainer of my life;
And if I am presumptuous so to do,
   In spite of all their bitterness and strife,
It is because your gentle Love's one thought
   Is both to love and serve you loyally,
To count the worst that fate can do as naught,
   And to make *my* will with *your* will agree.
Someday you certainly will comprehend
   How steadfast is my purpose and how real,
Which is to do you pleasure until death,
Only to you, being subject: in which faith
I do indeed most fervently intend
To live and die. To this I set my seal.

MARY STUART, QUEEN OF SCOTS

Sonnet 34

Why didst thou promise such a beauteous day,
And make me travel forth without my cloak,
To let base clouds o'ertake me in my way,
Hiding thy bravery in their rotten smoke?
'Tis not enough that through the cloud thou break,
To dry the rain on my storm-beaten face,
For no man well of such a salve can speak
That heals the wound and cures not the disgrace:
Nor can thy shame give physic to my grief;
Though thou repent, yet I have still the loss:
The offender's sorrow lends but weak relief
To him that bears the strong offence's cross.
   Ah, but those tears are pearl which thy love sheds,
   And they are rich and ransom all ill deeds.

WILLIAM SHAKESPEARE

Sonnet 140

Be wise as thou art cruel; do not press
My tongue-tied patience with too much disdain;
Lest sorrow lend me words, and words express
The manner of my pity-wanting pain.
If I might teach thee wit, better it were,
Though not to love, yet, love, to tell me so;
As testy sick men, when their deaths be near,
No news but health from their physicians know;
For, if I should despair, I should grow mad,
And in my madness might speak ill of thee:
Now this ill-wresting world is grown so bad,
Mad slanderers by mad ears believèd be.
   That I may not be so, nor thou belied,
   Bear thine eyes straight, though thy proud heart go wide.

WILLIAM SHAKESPEARE

To Sleep

O soft embalmer of the still midnight!
    Shutting, with careful fingers and benign,
Our gloom-pleased eyes, embower'd from the light,
    Enshaded in forgetfulness divine;
O soothest Sleep! if so it please thee, close,
    In midst of this thine hymn, my willing eyes,
Or wait the amen, ere thy poppy throws
    Around my bed its lulling charities;
Then save me, or the passèd day will shine
Upon my pillow, breeding many woes;
    Save me from curious conscience, that still lords
Its strength in darkness, burrowing like a mole;
    Turn the key deftly in the oilèd wards,
And seal the hushèd casket of my soul.

JOHN KEATS

As proper mode of quenching legal lust

As proper mode of quenching legal lust,
    A Roué takes unto Himself a Wife:
'Tis Cheaper when the bones begin to rust,
And there's no other Woman you can trust;
But, mind you, in return, Law says you must
    Provide her with the physical means of life:
And then the blindest beast may wallow and roll;
The twain are One flesh, never mind the Soul:
You may not cruelly beat her, but are free
To violate the life in sanctuary;
In virgin soil renew old seeds of Crime
To blast eternity as well as time:
    She must show black and blue, or no divorce
    Is granted by the Law of Physical Force.

GERALD MASSEY

She, to Him – 1

When you shall see me in the toils of Time,
My lauded beauties carried off from me,
My eyes no longer stars as in their prime,
My name forgot of Maiden Fair and Free;

When, in your being, heart concedes to mind,
And judgment, though you scarce its process know,
Recalls the excellencies I once enshrined,
And you are irked that they have withered so:

Remembering mine the loss is, not the blame,
That Sportsman Time but rears his brood to kill,
Knowing me in my soul the very same –
One who would die to spare you touch of ill! –
Will you not grant to old affection's claim
The hand of friendship down Life's sunless hill?

                                        THOMAS HARDY

She, to Him – 2

Perhaps, long hence, when I have passed away,
Some other's feature, accent, thought like mine,
Will carry you back to what I used to say,
And bring some memory of your love's decline.

Then you may pause awhile and think, 'Poor jade!'
And yield a sigh to me – as ample due,
Not as the tittle of a debt unpaid
To one who could resign her all to you –

And thus reflecting, you will never see
That your thin thought, in two small words conveyed,
Was no such fleeting phantom-thought to me,
But the Whole Life wherein my part was played;
And you amid its fitful masquerade
A Thought – as I in your life seem to be!

                                        THOMAS HARDY

She, to Him — 3

I will be faithful to thee; aye, I will!
And Death shall choose me with a wondering eye
That he did not discern and domicile
One his by right ever since that last Good-bye!

I have no care for friends, or kin, or prime
Of manhood who deal gently with me here;
Amid the happy people of my time
Who work their love's fulfilment, I appear

Numb as a vane that cankers on its point,
True to the wind that kissed ere canker came:
Despised by souls of Now, who would disjoint
The mind from memory, making Life all aim,

My old dexterities in witchery gone,
And nothing left for Love to look upon.

                                        THOMAS HARDY

Sonnets from Modern Love

1

By this he knew she wept with waking eyes:
    That, at his hand's light quiver by her head,
    The strange low sobs that shook their common bed
Were called into her with a sharp surprise,
And strangled mute, like little gaping snakes,
    Dreadfully venomous to him. She lay
    Stone-still, and the long darkness flowed away
With muffled pulses. Then, as midnight makes
Her giant heart of memory and tears
    Drink the pale drug of silence, and so beat
    Sleep's heavy measure, they from head to feet
Were moveless, looking through their dead black years,
By vain regret scrawled over the blank wall.
    Like sculptured effigies they might be seen
    Upon their marriage-tomb, the sword between;
Each wishing for the sword that severs all.

2

It ended, and the morrow brought the task.
    Her eyes were guilty gates, that let him in
    By shutting all too zealous for their sin:
Each sucked a secret, and each wore a mask.
But, oh, the bitter taste her beauty had!
    He sickened as at breath of poison-flowers:
    A languid humour stole among the hours,
And if their smiles encountered, he went mad.
And raged deep inward, till the light was brown
    Before his vision, and the world, forgot,
    Looked wicked as some old dull murder-spot.
A star with lurid beams, she seemed to crown
The pit of infamy: and then again
    He fainted on his vengefulness, and strove
    To ape the magnanimity of love,
And smote himself, a shuddering heap of pain.

16

In our old shipwrecked days there was an hour,
When in the firelight steadily aglow,
Joined slackly, we beheld the red chasm grow
Among the clicking coals. Our library-bower
That eve was left to us: and hushed we sat
As lovers to whom Time is whispering.
From sudden-opened doors we heard them sing:
The nodding elders mixed good wine with chat.
Well knew we that Life's greatest treasure lay
With us, and of it was our talk. 'Ah, yes!
Love dies!' I said: I never thought it less.
She yearned to me that sentence to unsay.
Then when the fire domed blackening, I found
Her cheek was salt against my kiss, and swift
Up the sharp scale of sobs her breast did lift: —
Now am I haunted by that taste! that sound!

17

At dinner, she is hostess, I am host.
Went the feast ever cheerfuller? She keeps
The Topic over intellectual deeps
In buoyancy afloat. They see no ghost.
With sparkling surface-eyes we ply the ball:
It is in truth a most contagious game:
HIDING THE SKELETON, shall be its name.
Such play as this, the devils might appal!
But here's the greater wonder; in that we
Enamoured of an acting nought can tire,
Each other, like true hypocrites, admire;
Warm-lighted looks, Love's ephemerioe,
Shoot gaily o'er the dishes and the wine.
We waken envy of our happy lot.
Fast, sweet, and golden, shows the marriage-knot.
Dear guests, you now have seen Love's corpse-light shine.

30

What are we first? First, animals; and next
Intelligences at a leap; on whom
Pale lies the distant shadow of the tomb,
And all that draweth on the tomb for text.
Into which state comes Love, the crowning sun:
Beneath whose light the shadow loses form.
We are the lords of life, and life is warm.
Intelligence and instinct now are one.
But Nature says: 'My children most they seem
When they least know me: therefore I decree
That they shall suffer.' Swift doth young Love flee,
And we stand wakened, shivering from our dream.
Then if we study Nature we are wise.
Thus do the few who live but with the day:
The scientific animals are they. –
Lady, this is my sonnet to your eyes.

45

It is the season of the sweet wild rose,
My Lady's emblem in the heart of me!
So golden-crownèd shines she gloriously,
And with that softest dream of blood she glows:
Mild as an evening heaven round Hesper bright!
I pluck the flower, and smell it, and revive
The time when in her eyes I stood alive.
I seem to look upon it out of Night.
Here's Madam, stepping hastily. Her whims
Bid her demand the flower, which I let drop.
As I proceed, I feel her sharply stop,
And crush it under heel with trembling limbs.
She joins me in a cat-like way, and talks
Of company, and even condescends
To utter laughing scandal of old friends.
These are the summer days, and these our walks.

GEORGE MEREDITH

One day

Today I have been happy. All the day
   I held the memory of you, and wove
Its laughter with the dancing light o' the spray,
   And sowed the sky with tiny clouds of love,
And sent you following the white waves of sea,
   And crowned your head with fancies, nothing worth,
Stray buds from that old dust of misery,
   Being glad with a new foolish quiet mirth.

So lightly I played with those dark memories,
Just as a child, beneath the summer skies,
   Plays hour by hour with a strange shining stone,
For which (he knows not) towns were fire of old,
   And love has been betrayed, and murder done,
And great kings turned to a little bitter mould.

RUPERT BROOKE

Unfortunate

Heart, you are restless as a paper scrap
   That's tossed down dusty pavements by the wind;
   Saying, 'She is most wise, patient and kind.
Between the small hands folded in her lap
Surely a shamed head may bow down at length,
   And find forgiveness where the shadows stir
About her lips, and wisdom in her strength,
   Peace in her peace. Come to her, come to her!' . . .

She will not care. She'll smile to see me come,
   So that I think all Heaven in flower to fold me.
   She'll give me all I ask, kiss me and hold me,
     And open wide upon that holy air
The gates of peace, and take my tiredness home,
     Kinder than God. But, heart, she will not care.

RUPERT BROOKE

Because I know

Because I know that there is that in me
   Of which thou shouldst be proud, and not ashamed, –
Because I feel one made *thy* choice should be
   Not even by fools and slanderers rashly blamed, –
Because I fear, howe'er thy soul may strive
   Against the weakness of that inward pain,
The falsehoods which my enemies contrive
   Not always seek to wound thine ear in vain, –
Therefore I sometimes weep, when I should smile,
   At all the vain frivolity and sin
Which those who know me not (yet me revile) –
   My would-be judges – cast my actions in;
But else their malice hath nor sting nor smart –
For I appeal from them, Beloved, to thine own heart!

                  CAROLINE NORTON

The Second Wife

She knows, being woman, that for him she holds
The space kept for the second blossoming,
Unmixed with dreams, held tightly in the folds
Of the accepted and long-proper thing –
She, duly loved; and he, proud of her looks
Shy of her wit. And of that other she knows
She had a slim throat, a nice taste in books,
And grew petunias in squat garden rows.
Thus knowing all, she feels both safe and strange;
Safe in his life, of which she has a share;
Safe in her undisturbed, cool, equal place,
In the sweet commonness that will not change;
And strange, when, at the door, in the spring air,
She hears him sigh, old Aprils in his face.

              LIZETTE WOODWORTH REESE

A Flower of Mullein

I am too near, too clear a thing for you,
A flower of mullein in a crack of wall,
The villagers half-see, or not at all,
Part of the weather, like the wind or dew.
You love to pluck the different, and find
Stuff for your joy in cloudy loveliness;
You love to fumble at a door, and guess
At some strange happening that may wait behind.
Yet life is full of tricks, and it is plain,
That men drift back to some worn field or roof,
To grip at comfort in a room, a stair,
To warm themselves at some flower down a lane:
You, too, may long, grown tired of the aloof,
For the sweet surety of the common air.

                              LIZETTE WOODWORTH REESE

In our content

In our content, before the autumn came
To shower sallow droppings on the mould,
Sometimes you have permitted me to fold
Your grief in swaddling-bands, and smile to name
Yourself my infant, with an infant's claim
To utmost adoration as of old,
Suckled with kindness, fondled from the cold,
And loved beyond philosophy or shame.

I dreamt I was the mother of a son
Who had deserved a manger for a crib;
Torn from your body, furnished from your rib,
I am the daughter of your skeleton,
Born of your bitter and excessive pain:
I shall not dream you are my child again.

                              ELINOR WYLIE

Some eyes condemn

Some eyes condemn the earth they gaze upon:
Some wait patiently till they know far more
Than earth can tell them: some laugh at the whole
As folly of another's making: one
I knew that laughed because he saw, from core
To rind, not one thing worth the laugh his soul
Had ready at waking: some eyes have begun
With laughing; some stand startled at the door.

Others, too, I have seen rest, question, roll,
Dance, shoot. And many I have loved watching.
    Some
I could not take my eyes from till they turned
And loving died. I had not found my goal.
But thinking of your eyes, dear, I become
Dumb: for they flamed and it was me they burned.

EDWARD THOMAS

5

FAITH

A prayer

Grant, I thee pray, such heat into mine heart
That to this love of thine may be equ'all;
Grant me from Satan's service to astart,
With whom me rueth so long to have been thrall;
Grant me, good Lord and Creator of all,
The flame to quench of all sinful desire
And in thy love set all mine heart afire.

That when the journey of this deadly life
My silly ghost hath finishèd, and thence
Departen must without his fleshly wife,
Alone into his Lordès high pres'ence,
He may thee find, O well of indulg'ence,
In thy lordship not as a lord, but rather
As a very tender, loving father.

SIR THOMAS MORE

The Lessons of Nature

Of this fair volume which we World do name
    If we the sheets and leaves could turn with care,
Of Him who it corrects, and did it frame,
    We clear might read the art and wisdom rare:

Find out His power which wildest powers doth tame,
    His providence extending everywhere,
    His justice which proud rebels doth not spare,
In every page, no period of the same.

But silly we, like foolish children, rest
    Well pleased with colour'd vellum, leaves of gold,
Fair dangling ribbands, leaving what is best,
    On the great Writer's sense ne'er taking hold;

Or if by chance we stay our minds on aught,
It is some picture on the margin wrought.

WILLIAM DRUMMOND

Batter my heart

Batter my heart, three-personed God; for you
As yet but knock, breathe, shine, and seek to mend.
That I may rise and stand, o'erthrow me, and bend
Your force to break, blow, burn, and make me new.
I, like an usurped town to another due,
Labour to admit you, but Oh, to no end.
Reason, your viceroy in me, me should defend,
But is captived, and proves weak or untrue.
Yet dearly I love you and would be lovèd fain,
But am betrothed unto your enemy.
Divorce me, untie, or break that knot again,
Take me to you, imprison me, for I,
Except you enthrall me, never shall be free,
Nor ever chaste, except you ravish me.

                                        JOHN DONNE

At the round earth's imagin'd corners, blow

At the round earth's imagin'd corners, blow
Your trumpets, Angells, and arise, arise
From death, you numberlesse infinities
Of soules, and to your scattred bodies 'goe,
All whom the flood did, and fire shall o'erthrow,
All whom warre, dearth, age, agues, tyrannies,
Despaire, law, chance, hath slaine, and you whose eyes
Shall behold God, and never tast death's woe.
But let them sleepe, Lord, and mee mourne a space.
For, if above all these, my sinnes abound,
'Tis late to aske abundance of thy grace,
When wee are there; here on this lowly ground,
Teach mee how to repent; for that's as good
As if thou hadst seal'd my pardon, with thy blood.

                                        JOHN DONNE

Thou hast made me

Thou hast made me; And shall thy worke decay?
Repaire me now, for now mine end doth haste,
I runne to death, and death meets me as fast,
And all my pleasures are like yesterday;
I dare not move my dimme eyes any way,
Despaire behind, and death before doth cast
Such terrour, and my feeble flesh doth waste
By sinne in it, which it t'wards hell doth weigh;
Onely thou art above, and when towards thee
By thy leave I can looke, I rise againe;
But our old subtle foe so tempteth me,
That not one hour myselfe I can sustaine;
Thy Grace may wing me to prevent his art,
And thou like Adamant draw mine iron heart.

JOHN DONNE

Death be not proud

Death be not proud, though some have called thee
Mighty and dreadfull, for, thou art not soe,
For, those, whom thou think'st, thou dost overthrow,
Die not, poore death, nor yet canst thou kill mee.
From rest and sleepe, which but thy pictures bee,
Much pleasure, then from thee, much more must flow,
And soonest our best men with thee doe goe,
Best of their bones, and soules deliverie.
Thou art slave to Fate, Chance, kings, and desperate men,
And dost with poyson, warre, and sicknesse dwell,
And poppie, or charmes can make us sleepe as well,
And better than thy stroake; why swell'st thou then?
One short sleepe past, wee wake eternally,
And death shall be no more; death, thou shalt die.

JOHN DONNE

To God the Father

Great God, within whose simple essence we
Nothing but that which is thyself can find;
When on thyself thou didst reflect thy mind,
Thy thought was God, and took the form of thee:
And when this God, thus born, thou lov'st, and he
Loved thee again, with passion of like kind
(As lovers' sighs which meet become one wind),
Both breathed one sprite of equal deity.
Eternal Father, whence these two do come
And wilt the title of my father have,
And heavenly knowledge in my mind engrave,
That it thy son's true Image may become:
    And cense my heart with sighs of holy love,
    That it the temple of the Sprite may prove.

HENRY CONSTABLE

Redemption

Having been tenant long to a rich Lord,
    Not thriving, I resolvèd to be bold,
    And make a suit unto him, to afford
A new small-rented lease, and cancel th' old.

In Heaven at his manor I him sought:
    They told me there, that he was lately gone
    About some land, which he had dearly bought
Long since on earth, to take possessi'on.

I straight return'd, and knowing his great birth,
    Sought him accordingly in great resorts;
    In cities, theatres, gardens, parks, and courts:
At length I heard a ragged noise and mirth

    Of thieves and murderers: there I him espied,
    Who straight, *Your suit is granted*, said, and died.

GEORGE HERBERT

The Son

Let foreign nations of their language boast,
What fine variety each tongue affords:
I like our language, as our men and coast:
Who cannot dress it well, want wit, not words.
How neatly do we give one only name
To parents' issue and the sun's bright star!
A son is light and fruit; a fruitful flame
Chasing the father's dimness, carried far
From the first man in th'East, to fresh and new
Western discoveries of posterity.
So in one word our Lord's humility
We turn upon him in a sense most true:
   For what Christ once in humbleness began,
   We him in glory call, *The Son of Man*.

GEORGE HERBERT

Holy Baptism

As he that sees a dark and shady grove,
   Stays not, but looks beyond it on the sky;
   So when I view my sins, mine eyes remove
More backward still, and to that water fly,

Which is above the heavens, whose spring and vent
   Is in my dear Redeemer's piercèd side.
   O blessed streams! either ye do prevent
And stop our sins from growing thick and wide,

Or else give tears to drown them, as they grow.
   In you Redemption measures all my time,
   And spreads the plaster equal to the crime:
You taught the book of life my name, that so,

   Whatever future sins should me miscall,
   Your first acquaintance might discredit all.

GEORGE HERBERT

Sin

Lord, with what care hast thou begirt us round!
    Parents first season us: then schoolmasters
    Deliver us to laws; they send us bound
To rules of reason, holy messengers,

Pulpits and Sundays, sorrow dogging sin,
    Afflictions sorted, anguish of all sizes,
    Fine nets and stratagems to catch us in,
Bibles laid open, millions of surprises,

Blessings beforehand, ties of gratefulness,
    The sound of glory ringing in our ears;
    Without, our shame; within, our consciences;
Angels and grace, eternal hopes and fears.

    Yet all these fences and their whole array
    One cunning bosom-sin blows quite away.

GEORGE HERBERT

Prayer

Prayer, the Church's banquet, Angel's age.
    God's breath in man returning to his birth,
    The soul in paraphrase, heart in pilgrimage,
The Christian plummet sounding heaven and earth;

Engine against th' Almighty, sinner's tower,
    Reversèd thunder, Christ-side-piercing spear,
    The six days' world transposing in an hour,
A kind of tune, which all things hear and fear;

Softness, and peace, and joy, and love, and bliss,
    Exalted Manna, gladness of the best,
    Heaven in ordinary, men well drest,
The Milky Way, the bird of Paradise,

    Church-bells beyond the stars heard, the soul's blood,
    The land of spices, something understood.

GEORGE HERBERT

On his Blindness

When I consider how my light is spent
Ere half my days, in this dark world and wide,
And that one talent which is death to hide
lodged with me useless, though my soul more bent

To serve therewith my Maker, and present
My true account, lest He returning chide, –
Doth God exact day-labour, light denied?
I fondly ask: – But Patience, to prevent

That murmur, soon replies; God doth not need
Either man's work, or His own gifts: who best
Bear His mild yoke, they serve Him best: His state

Is kingly; thousands at His bidding speed
And post o'er land and ocean without rest: –
They also serve who only stand and wait.

JOHN MILTON

As kingfishers catch fire

As kingfishers catch fire, dragonflies dráw fláme;
As tumbled over rim in roundy wells
Stones ring; like each tucked string tells, each hung bell's
Bow swung finds tongue to fling out broad its name;
Each mortal thing does one thing and the same:
Deals out that being indoors each one dwells;
Selves — goes itself; *myself* it speaks and spells;
Crying Whát I dó is me: for that I came.

Í say móre: the just man justices;
Kéeps gráce: thát keeps all his goings graces;
Acts in God's eye what in God's eye he is —
Chríst — for Christ plays in ten thousand places,
Lovely in limbs, and lovely in eyes not his
To the Father through the features of men's faces.

GERARD MANLEY HOPKINS

The Windhover

To Christ our Lord

I caught this morning morning's minion, king-
   dom of daylight's dauphin, dapple-dawn-drawn Falcon,
      in his riding
   Of the rolling level underneath him steady air, and striding
High there, how he rung upon the rein of a wimpling wing
In his ecstasy! then off, off forth on swing,
   As a skate's heel sweeps smooth on a bow-bend:
      the hurl and gliding
   Rebuffed the big wind. My heart in hiding
Stirred for a bird, – the achieve of, the mastery of the thing!

Brute beauty and valour and act, oh, air, pride, plume, here
   Buckle! *And* the fire that breaks from thee then, a billion
Times told lovelier, more dangerous, O my chevalier!

   No wonder of it: shéer plod makes plough down sillion
Shine, and blue-bleak embers, ah my dear,
   Fall, gall themselves, and gash gold-vermilion.

GERARD MANLEY HOPKINS

The Starlight Night

Look at the stars! look, look up at the skies!
O look at all the fire-folk sitting in the air!
The bright boroughs, the circle-citadels there!
Down in dim woods the diamond delves! the elves'-e
The grey lawns cold where gold, where quickgold lie
Wind-beat whitebeam! airy abeles set on a flare!
Flake-doves sent floating forth at a farmyard scare!
Ah well! it is all a purcháse, all is a prize.

Buy then! bid then! – What? – Prayer, patience, alm
Look, look: a May-mess, like on orchard boughs!
Look! March-bloom, like on mealed-with-yellow
These are indeed the barn; withindoors house
The shocks. This piece-bright paling shuts the spous
Christ home, Christ and his mother and all his hallows.

GERARD MANLEY HOPKINS

God's Grandeur

The world is charged with the grandeur of God.
   It will flame out, like shining from shook foil;
   It gathers to a greatness, like the ooze of oil
Crushed. Why do men then now not reck his rod?
Generations have trod, have trod, have trod;
   And all is seared with trade; bleared, smeared with toil;
   And wears man's smudge and shares man's smell: the soil
Is bare now, nor can foot feel, being shod.

And for all this, nature is never spent;
   There lives the dearest freshness deep down things;
And though the last lights off the black West went
   Oh, morning, at the brown brink eastward, springs
Because the Holy Ghost over the bent
   World broods with warm breast and with ah! bright wings.

GERARD MANLEY HOPKINS

Thou art indeed just

Thou art indeed just, Lord, if I contend
With thee; but, sir, so what I plead is just.
Why do sinners' ways prosper? and why must
Disappointment all I endeavour end?
   Wert thou my enemy, O thou my friend,
How wouldst thou worse, I wonder, than thou dost
Defeat, thwart me? Oh, the sots and thralls of lust
Do in spare hours more thrive than I that spend,
Sir, life upon thy cause. See, banks and brakes
Now, leavèd how thick! lacèd they are again
With fretty chervil, look, and fresh wind shakes
Them; birds build – but not I build; no, but strain,
Time's eunuch, and not breed one work that wakes.
Mine, O thou lord of life, send my roots rain.

GERARD MANLEY HOPKINS

Let me be to Thee as the circling bird

Let me be to Thee as the circling bird,
Or bat with tender and air-crisping wings
That shapes in half-light his departing rings,
From both of whom a changeless note is heard.
I have found my music in a common word,
Trying each pleasurable throat that sings
And every praised sequence of sweet strings,
And know infallibly which I preferred.
The authentic cadence was discovered late
Which ends those only strains that I approve,
And other science all gone out of date
And minor sweetness scarce made mention of:
I have found the dominant of my range and state –
Love, O my God, to call Thee Love and Love.

GERARD MANLEY HOPKINS

Sonnet

The azured vault, the crystal circles bright,
The gleaming fiery torches powdered there;
The changing round, the shining beamy light,
The sad and bearded fires, the monsters fair;
The prodigies appearing in the air;
The rearding thunders and the blustering winds;
The fowls in hue and shape and nature rare,
The pretty notes that winged musicians finds;
In earth, the savoury flowers, the metalled minds,
The wholesome herbs, the hautie pleasant trees,
The silver streams, the beasts of sundry kinds,
The bounded roars and fishes of the seas, –
      All these, for teaching man, the Lord did frame
      To do his will whose glory shines in them.

KING JAMES I

Decay of Piety

Oft have I seen, ere Time had ploughed my cheek,
Matrons and Sires – who, punctual to the call
Of their loved Church, on fast or festival
Through the long year the House of Prayer would seek:
By Christmas snows, by visitation bleak
Of Easter winds, unscared, from hut or hall
They came to lowly bench or sculptured stall,
But with one fervour of devotion meek.
I see the places where they once were known,
And ask, surrounded even by kneeling crowds,
Is ancient Piety for ever flown?
Alas! even then they seemed like fleecy clouds
That, struggling through the western sky, have won
Their pensive light from a departed sun!

WILLIAM WORDSWORTH

The Good Shepherd with the Kid

He saves the sheep, the goats he doth not save.
So rang Tertullian's sentence, on the side
Of that unpitying Phrygian sect which cried:
'Him can no fount of fresh forgiveness lave,

'Who sins, once wash'd by the baptismal wave.' —
So spake the fierce Tertullian. But she sigh'd,
The infant Church! of love she felt the tide
Stream on her from her Lord's yet recent grave

And then she smiled; and in the Catacombs,
With eye suffused but heart inspired true,
On those walls subterranean, where she hid

Her head 'mid ignominy, death, and tombs,
She her Good Shepherd's hasty image drew —
And on his shoulders, not a lamb, a kid.

MATTHEW ARNOLD

Sonnet

On hearing the Dies Irae *sung in the Sistine Chapel*

Nay, Lord, not thus! white lilies in the spring,
    Sad olive-groves, or silver-breasted dove,
    Teach me more clearly of Thy life and love
Than terrors of red flame and thundering.
The hillside vines dear memories of Thee bring:
    A bird at evening flying to its nest
    Tells me of One who had no place of rest:
I think it is of Thee the sparrows sing.
Come rather on some autumn afternoon,
    When red and brown are burnished on the leaves,
    And the fields echo to the gleaner's song,
Come when the splendid fulness of the moon,
    Looks down upon the rows of golden sheaves,
    And reap Thy harvest: we have waited long.

OSCAR WILDE

Chartres Windows

Colour fulfils where Music has no power:
    By each man's light the unjudging glass betrays
All men's surrender, each man's holiest hour
    And all the lit confusion of our days –
Purfled with iron, traced in dusk and fire,
    Challenging ordered Time who, at the last,
    Shall bring it, grozed and leaded and wedged fast,
To the cold stone that curbs or crowns desire.
Yet on the pavement that all feet have trod –
    Even as the Spirit, in her deeps and heights,
Turns only, and that voiceless, to her God –
    There falls no tincture from those anguished lights.
And Heaven's one light, behind them, striking through
Blazons what each man dreamed no other knew.

RUDYARD KIPLING

Lucifer in Starlight

On a starred night Prince Lucifer uprose.
Tired of his dark dominion swung the fiend
Above the rolling ball in cloud part screened,
Where sinners hugged their spectre of repose.
Poor prey to his hot fit of pride were those
And now upon his western wing he leaned
Now his huge bulk o'er Afric's sands careened,
Now the black planet shadowed Arctic snows.
Soaring through wider zones that pricked his scars
With memory of the old revolt from Awe,
He reached a middle height, and at the stars,
Which are the brain of heaven, he looked, and sank.
Around the ancient track marched, rank on rank,
The army of unalterable law.

GEORGE MEREDITH

Maundy Thursday

Between the brown hands of a server-lad
The silver cross was offered to be kissed.
The men came up, lugubrious, but not sad,
And knelt reluctantly, half-prejudiced.
(And kissing, kissed the emblem of a creed.)
Then mourning women knelt; meek mouths they had,
(And kissed the Body of the Christ indeed.)
Young children came, with eager lips and glad.
(These kissed a silver doll, immensely bright.)
Then I, too, knelt before that acolyte.
Above the crucifix I bent my head:
The Christ was thin, and cold, and very dead:
And yet I bowed, yea, kissed – my lips did cling.
(I kissed the warm live hand that held the thing.)

WILFRED OWEN

To a Medieval Workman: Winchester

Here, where aspiring arch or pillar raises
Its marble anthem to the timeless sky,
My thought slips back to you who wrought God's praises
With singing mind and grave, unerring eye.
I see you carving out your cosmic wonder –
Some gay device of birds or fleur-de-lys –
The teeming universe all yours to plunder
And chisel from rough stone's austerity.

Today a blind age gropes for that untainted
Vision the soul's humility discerned
Eight centuries past, when skilled hands' patient art
Shaped this saint's head, or Mary's mantle painted:
Lend us your faith-filled eyes, O you who learned
The secret wisdom of the child-like heart!

MARGARET WILLY

The Cathedral Verger

Pacing with leisured tread the echoing nave
Between these soundless, frozen waterfalls,
He sees the fingering dawn, or winter's grave
Snowlight transfigure time-beleaguered walls;
And, wondering, knows this re-creating snow
Chiselling anew carved angel, beast or flower,
The same which lit, six centuries ago,
The cowled monk's vigil through each creeping hour.

From starry fresco, vaulted roof and pier,
From century-trodden flags beneath his feet,
They stir, and speak within his living bone –
Friends who, long dust, enslave this sentient ear,
And bind the warm heart, to its last faint beat,
To this still, sculptured loveliness of stone.

MARGARET WILLY

6

DESPAIR

The Lover Compareth his State to a Ship in Perilous Storm Tossed on the Sea

My galley, chargèd with forgetfulness,
Thorough sharp seas in winter nights doth pass
'Tween rock and rock, and eke my foe, alas,
That is my lord, steereth with cruelness;
And every hour, a thought in readiness,
As though that death were light in such a case;
An endless wind doth tear the sail apace
Of forcèd sighs, and trusty fearfulness;
A rain of tears, a cloud of dark disdain,
Hath done the wearied cords great hinderance;
Wreathèd with error and eke with ignorance,
The stars be hid that led me to this pain.
   Drownèd is reason that should me comfort,
   And I remain, despairing of the port.

SIR THOMAS WYATT

Rime 57

Ever myn happe is slack and slo in commyng,
  Desir encresing, myn hope uncertain,
  That leve it or wayt it doeth me like pain,
And Tigre like, swift it is in parting.
Alas, the snow shal be black and scalding,
  The See waterles, fisshe in the moyntain,
  The Tamys shall retorne back into his fountain,
  And where he rose the sonne shall take lodging,
Ere that I in this fynde peace or quyetenes,
  Or that love or my lady right wisely
  Leve to conspire again me wrongfully;
And if that I have after suche bitternes
  Any thing swete, my mouth is owte of tast,
  That all my trust and travaill is but wast.

SIR THOMAS WYATT

Rime 269

From the Italian of Petrarch

The piller pearisht is whearto I Lent
  The strongest staye of myne unquyet mynde;
  The lyke of it no man agayne can fynde
  From East to west still seking though he went.
To myne unhappe, for happe away hath rent
  Of all my joye the vearye bark and rynde;
  And I (alas) by chaunce am thus assynde
  Dearlye to moorne till death do it relent.
But syns that thus it is by destenye
  What can I more but have a wofull hart,
  My penne in playnt, my voyce in wofull crye,
My mynde in woe, my bodye full of smart,
  And I my self my self alwayes to hate
  Till dreadfull death do ease my dolefull state?

SIR THOMAS WYATT

A Complaint by Night of the Lover not Beloved

Alas! so all things now do hold their peace;
Heaven and earth disturbèd in no thing:
The beasts, the air, the birds their song do cease;
The nightès chare the stars about doth bring:
Calm is the sea; the waves work less and less:
So am not l, whom love, alas, doth wring,
Bringing before my face the great increase
Of my desires, whereat I weep and sing,
In joy and woe, as in a doubtful ease:
For my sweet thoughts sometime do pleasure bring;
But by and by, the cause of my disease
Gives me a pang, that inwardly doth sting,
   When that I think what grief it is again,
   To live and lack the thing should rid my pain.

HENRY HOWARD, EARL OF SURREY

Description of Spring,
Wherein each thing Renews,
save only the Lover

The soote season, that bud and bloom forth brings,
With green hath clad the hill and eke the vale:
The nightingale with feathers new she sings;
The turtle to her make hath told her tale.
Summer is come, for every spray now springs:
The hart hath hung his old head on the pale;
The buck in brake his winter coat he flings;
The fishes float with new repairèd scale;
The adder all her slough away she slings;
The swift swallow pursueth the flies smale;
The busy bee her honey now she mings;
Winter is worn that was the flowers' bale.
   And thus I see among these pleasant things
   Each care decays; and yet my sorrow springs.

HENRY HOWARD, EARL OF SURREY

If ever Sorrow spoke

If ever Sorrow spoke from soul that loves,
As speaks a spirit in a man possessed,
In me her spirit speaks, my soul it moves,
Whose sigh-swoln words breed whirlwinds in my breast:
Or like the echo of a passing bell
Which, sounding on the water, seems to howl,
So rings my heart a fearful heavy knell,
And keeps all night in consort with the owl:
My cheeks with a thin ice of tears is clad,
Mine eyes, like morning stars, are bleared and red,
What resteth then but I be raging mad,
To see that she, my care's chief conduit-head,
    When all streams else help quench my burning heart,
    Shuts up her springs, and will no grace impart.

HENRY CONSTABLE

Like as a ship that through the ocean wide

Like as a ship that through the ocean wide
    By conduct of some star doth make her way,
Whenas a storm hath dimmed her trusty guide,
    Out of her course doth wander far astray:
    So I whose star, that wont with her bright ray
Me to direct, with clouds is overcast,
    Do wander now in darkness and dismay,
Through hidden perils round about me placed.
Yet hope I well, that when this storm is past,
    My Helicé, the lodestar of my life,
Will shine again, and look on me at last,
    With lovely light to clear my cloudy grief.
Till then I wander, care-full, comfortless,
In secret sorrow and sad pensiveness.

EDMUND SPENSER

Fly hence O! joy

Fly hence O! joy noe longer heere abide
   Too great thy pleasures ar for my dispaire
   To looke on, losses now must prove my fare
   Who nott long since, on better foode relide;

Butt foole, how oft had I heavns changing spide
   Beefore of my owne fate I could have care,
   Yett now past time, I can too late beeware
   When nothing's left butt sorrowes faster tyde;

While I injoy'd that sunn whose sight did lend
   Mee joy, I thought, that day, could have noe end
   Butt soone a night came cloth'd in absence darke,

Absence more sad, more bitter then is gall
   Or death, when on true lovers itt doth fall
   Whose fires of love, disdaine rests poorer sparke.

LADY MARY WROTH

From Pamphilia to Amphilanthus

Griefe, killing griefe: have nott my torments binn
  Allreddy great, and strong enough: butt still
  Thou dost increase, nay glory in mine all,
  And woes new past affresh new woes beeginn!

Am I the only purchase thou canst winn?
  Was I ordain'd to give dispaire her fill
  Or fittest I should mounte misfortunes hill
  Who in the plaine of joy can-nott live in?

If itt bee soe: Griefe come as wellcome ghest
  Since I must suffer, for an others rest:
  Yett this good griefe, lett mee intreat of thee,

Use still thy force, butt nott from those I love
  Lett mee all paines and lasting torments prove
  Soe I miss thes, lay all thy waits on mee.

                                        LADY MARY WROTH

Sonnet 66

Tired with all these, for restful death I cry,
  As, to behold desert a beggar born,
  And needy nothing trimm'd in jollity,
  And purest faith unhappily forsworn,
  And gilded honour shamefully misplaced,
  And maiden virtue rudely strumpeted,
  And right perfection wrongfully disgraced,
  And strength by limping sway disabled,
  And art made tongue-tied by authority,
  And folly, doctor-like, controlling skill,
  And simple truth miscall'd simplicity,
  And captive good attending captain ill:
    Tired with all these, from these would I be gone,
    Save that, to die, I leave my love alone.

                                    WILLIAM SHAKESPEARE

Sonnet 129

The expense of spirit in a waste of shame
Is lust in action; and till action, lust
Is perjured, murderous, bloody, full of blame,
Savage, extreme, rude, cruel, not to trust;
Enjoy'd no sooner but despisèd straight;
Past reason hunted; and no sooner had,
Past reason hated, as a swallowed bait,
On purpose laid to make the taker mad:
Mad in pursuit, and in possession so;
Had, having, and in quest to have, extreme;
A bliss in proof, and proved, a very woe;
Before, a joy proposed; behind, a dream.
    All this the world well knows; yet none knows well
    To shun the heaven that leads men to this hell.

WILLIAM SHAKESPEARE

Surprised by joy

Surprised by joy – impatient as the Wind
I turned to share the transport – Oh! with whom
But Thee, deep buried in the silent tomb,
That spot which no vicissitude can find?
Love, faithful love, recalled thee to my mind –
But how could I forget thee? Through what power,
Even for the least division of an hour,
Have I been so beguilèd as to be blind
To my most grievous loss! – That thought's return
Was the worst pang that sorrow ever bore,
Save one, one only, when I stood forlorn,
Knowing my heart's best treasure was no more;
That neither present time, nor years unborn
Could to my sight that heavenly face restore.

WILLIAM WORDSWORTH

Work without Hope

All Nature seems at work. Slugs leave their lair –
The bees are stirring – birds are on the wing –
And Winter slumbering in the open air,
Wears on his smiling face a dream of Spring!
And I the while, the sole unbusy thing,
Nor honey make, nor pair, nor build, nor sing.

    Yet well I ken the banks where amaranths blow,
Have traced the fount whence streams of nectar flow.
Bloom, O ye amaranths! bloom for whom ye may,
For me ye bloom not! Glide, rich streams, away!
With lips unbrightened, wreathless brow, I stroll:
And would you learn the spells that drowse my soul?
Work without Hope draws nectar in a sieve,
And Hope without an object cannot live.

SAMUEL TAYLOR COLERIDGE

Farewell to Love

Farewell, sweet Love! yet blame you not my truth;
   More fondly ne'er did mother eye her child
Than I your form: *yours* were my hopes of youth,
   And as *you* shaped my thoughts I sighed or smiled.

While most were wooing wealth, or gaily swerving
   To pleasure's secret haunts, and some apart
Stood strong in pride, self-conscious of deserving,
   To you I gave my whole weak wishing heart.

And when I met the maid that realised
   Your fair creations, and had won her kindness,
Say, but for her if aught on earth I prized!
   Your dreams alone I dreamt, and caught your blindness.

O grief! – but farewell, Love! I will go play me
With thoughts that please me less, and less betray me.

SAMUEL TAYLOR COLERIDGE

I wake and feel the fell of dark

I wake and feel the fell of dark, not day.
What hours, O what black hoürs we have spent
This night! what sights you, heart, saw, ways you went!
And more must, in yet longer light's delay

With witness I speak this. But where I say
Hours I mean years, mean life. And my lament
Is cries countless, cries like dead letters sent
To dearest him that lives alas! away.

I am gall, I am heartburn. God's most deep decree
Bitter would have me taste: my taste was me;
Bones built in me, flesh filled, blood brimmed the curse.

Selfyeast of spirit a dull dough sours. I see
The lost are like this, and their scourge to be
As I am mine, their sweating selves; but worse.

GERARD MANLEY HOPKINS

To seem the stranger

To seem the stranger lies my lot, my life
Among strangers. Father and mother dear,
Brothers and sisters are in Christ not near
And he my peace/my parting, sword and strife.

England, whose honour Ō all my heart woos, wife
To my creating thought, would neither hear
Me, were I pleading, plead nor do I: I wear-
y of idle a being but by where wars are rife.

I am in Ireland now; now I am at a third
Remove. Not but in all removes I can
Kind love both give and get. Only what word

Wisest my heart breeds dark heaven's baffling ban
Bars or hell's spell thwarts. This to hoard unheard,
Heard unheeded, leaves me a lonely began.

GERARD MANLEY HOPKINS

No worst, there is none

No worst, there is none. Pitched past pitch of grief,
More pangs will, schooled at forepangs, wilder wring.
Comforter, where, where is your comforting?
Mary, mother of us, where is your relief?
My cries heave, herds-long; huggle in a main, a chief
Woe, world-sorrow; on an age-old anvil wince and sing –
Then lull, then leave off. Fury had shrieked 'No ling-
ering! Let me be fell: force I must be brief'.

O the mind, mind has mountains; cliffs of fall
Frightful, sheer, non-man-fathomed. Hold them cheap
May who ne'er hung there. Nor does long our small
Durance deal with that steep or deep. Here! creep,
Wretch, under a comfort serves in a whirlwind: all
Life death does end and each day dies with sleep.

GERARD MANLEY HOPKINS

Here have I been these one and twenty years

Here have I been these one and twenty years
Since first to Being's breeze my Soul unfurled
A voyager upon the wavy world
Half idling, half at work: – by empty fears
And emptier hopes, light mirth and fleeting tears
Tacking and tossed forever yet in vain
Now timidly retiring, now again
Carelessly, idly mingling with my peers.
Here have I been and done myself and other
E'en as much evil and as little good
As misused strength and guideless frailty could;
Here am I friendless and without a brother,
With faculties developed to no end,
Heart emptied, and scarce hoping to amend.

ARTHUR HUGH CLOUGH

Hap

If but some vengeful god would call to me
    From up the sky, and laugh: 'Thou suffering thing,
Know that thy sorrow is my ecstasy,
    That thy love's loss is my hate's profiting!'

Then would I bear it, clench myself, and die,
    Steeled by the sense of ire unmerited;
Half-eased in that a Powerfuller than I
    Had willed and meted me the tears I shed.

But not so. How arrives it joy lies slain,
    And why unblooms the best hope ever sown?
    Crass Casualty obstructs the sun and rain,
    And dicing Time for gladness casts a moan . . .
    These purblind Doomsters had as readily strown
Blisses about my pilgrimage as pain.

THOMAS HARDY

7

FAMILY LOVE

To his Son

Three things there be that prosper all apace
And flourish, while they grow asunder far;
But on a day, they meet all in a place,
And when they meet they one another mar.
And they be these: the Wood, the Weed, the Wag.
The Wood is that that makes the gallows tree;
The Weed is that that strings the hangman's bag;
The Wag, my pretty knave, betokens thee.
Now mark, dear boy – while these assemble not,
Green springs the tree, hemp grows, the wag is wild;
But when they meet, it makes the timber rot,
It frets the halter, and it chokes the child.
Then bless thee, and beware, and let us pray
We part not with thee at this meeting-day.

SIR WALTER RALEGH

On Receiving a Letter Informing Me
of the Birth of a Son

When they did greet me father, sudden awe
  Weigh'd down my spirit: I retired and knelt
  Seeking the throne of grace, but inly felt
No heavenly visitation upwards draw
My feeble mind, nor cheering ray impart.
  Ah me! before the Eternal Sire I brought
  Th' unquiet silence of confusèd thought
And shapeless feelings: my o'erwhelmèd heart
Trembled, and vacant tears stream'd down my face.
And now once more, O Lord! to thee I bend,
  Lover of souls! and groan for future grace,
That ere my babe youth's perilous maze have trod,
  Thy overshadowing Spirit may descend,
  And he be born again, a child of God.

SAMUEL TAYLOR COLERIDGE

To a Friend who Asked, How I Felt
when the Nurse Presented my Infant to Me

Charles! my slow heart was only sad, when first
  I scann'd that face of feeble infancy:
For dimly on my thoughtful spirit burst
  All I had been, and all my child might be!
But when I saw it on its mother's arm,
  And hanging at her bosom (she the while
  Bent o'er its features with a tearful smile)
Then I was thrill'd and melted, and most warm
Impress'd a father's kiss: and all beguil'd
  Of dark remembrance and presageful fear,
  I seem'd to see an angel-form appear –
'Twas even thine, belovèd woman mild!
  So for the mother's sake the child was dear,
And dearer was the mother for the child.

SAMUEL TAYLOR COLERIDGE

In Sight of the Town of Cockermouth

*(Where the Author was born, and his
Father's remains are laid)*

A point of life between my Parents' dust,
And yours, my buried Little-ones! am I;
And to those graves looking habitually
In kindred quiet I repose my trust.
Death to the innocent is more than just,
And, to the sinner, mercifully bent;
So may I hope, if truly I repent
And meekly bear the ills which bear I must:
And You, my Offspring! that do still remain,
Yet may outstrip me in the appointed race,
If e'er, through fault of mine, in mutual pain
We breathed together for a moment's space,
The wrong, by love provoked, let love arraign,
And only love keep in your hearts a place.

WILLIAM WORDSWORTH

To my Brothers

Small, busy flames play through the fresh-laid coals,
    And their faint cracklings o'er our silence creep
    Like whispers of the household gods that keep
A gentle empire o'er fraternal souls,
And while, for rhymes, I search around the poles,
    Your eyes are fix'd, as in poetic sleep
    Upon the lore so voluble and deep,
That aye at fall of night our care condoles.
This is your birth-day, Tom, and I rejoice
    That thus it passes smoothly, quietly.
Many such eves of gently whispering noise
    May we together pass, and calmly try
What are this world's true joys, – ere the great voice
    From its fair face shall bid our spirits fly.

JOHN KEATS

Brother and Sister

1

I cannot choose but think upon the time
When our two lives grew like two buds that kiss
At lightest thrill from the bee's swinging chime,
Because the one so near the other is.

He was the elder and a little man
Of forty inches, bound to show no dread,
And I the girl that puppy like now ran,
Now lagged behind my brother's larger tread.

I held him wise, and when he talked to me
Of snakes and birds, and which God loved the best,
I thought his knowledge marked the boundary
Where men grew blind, though angels knew the rest.

   If he said 'Hush!' I tried to hold my breath
   Wherever he said 'Come!' I stepped in faith.

2

Long years have left their writing on my brow,
But yet the freshness and the dew-fed beam
Of those young mornings are about me now,
When we two wandered toward the far-off stream

With rod and line. Our basket held a store
Baked for us only, and I thought with joy
That I should have my share, though he had more,
Because he was the elder and a boy.

The firmaments of daisies since to me
Have had those mornings in their opening eyes,
The bunchèd cowslip's pale transparency
Carries that sunshine of sweet memories,

   And wild-rose branches take their finest scent
   From those blest hours of infantine content.

3

Our mother bade us keep the trodden ways,
Stroked down my tippet, set my brother's frill,
Then with the benediction of her gaze
Clung to us lessening, and pursued us still

Across the homestead to the rookery elms,
Whose tall old trunks had each a grassy mound,
So rich for us, we counted them as realms
With varied products: here were earth-nuts found,

And here the Lady-fingers in deep shade;
Here sloping toward the Moat the rushes grew,
The large to split for pith, the small to braid;
While over all the dark rooks cawing flew,

And made a happy strange solemnity,
A deep-toned chant from life unknown to me.

4

Our meadow-path had memorable spots:
One where it bridged a tiny rivulet,
Deep hid my tangled blue Forget-me-nots;
And all along the waving grasses met

My little palm, or nodded to my cheek,
When flowers with upturned faces gazing drew
My wonder downward, seeming all to speak
With eyes of souls that dumbly heard and knew.

Then came the copse, where wild things rushed unseen,
And black-scathed grass betrayed the past abode
Of mystic gypsies, who still lurked between
Me and each hidden distance of the road.

A gypsy once had startled me at play
Blotting with her dark smile my sunny day.

5

Thus rambling we were schooled in deepest lore,
And learned the meanings that give words a soul,
The fear, the love, the primal passionate store,
Whose shaping impulses make manhood whole.

Those hours were seed to all my after good;
My infant gladness, through eye, ear, and touch,
Took easily as warmth a various food
To nourish the sweet skill of loving much.

For who in age shall roam the earth and find
Reasons for loving that will strike out love
With sudden rod from the hard year-pressèd mind?
Were reasons sown as thick as stars above,

  'Tis love must see them, as the eye sees light:
  Day is but Number to the darkened sight.

6

Our brown canal was endless to my thought;
And on its banks I sat in dreamy peace,
Unknowing how the good I loved was wrought,
Untroubled by the fear that it would cease.

Slowly the barges floated into view
Rounding a grassy hill to me sublime
With some Unknown beyond it, whither flew
The parting cuckoo toward a fresh spring time.

The wide-arched bridge, the scented elder-flowers,
The wondrous watery rings that died too soon,
The echoes of the quarry, the still hours
With white robe sweeping-on the shadeless noon,

  Were but my growing self, are part of me,
  My present Past, my root of piety.

7

Those long days measured by my little feet
Had chronicles which yield me many a text;
Where irony still finds an image meet
Of full-grown judgments in this world perplext.

One day my brother left me in high charge,
To mind the rod, while he went seeking bait,
And bade me, when I saw a nearing barge,
Snatch out the line, lest he should come too late.

Proud of the task, I watched with all my might
For one whole minute, till my eyes grew wide,
Till sky and earth took on a strange new light
And seemed a dream-world floating on some tide –

    A fair pavilioned boat for me alone
    Bearing me onward through the vast unknown.

8

But sudden came the barge's pitch-black prow,
Nearer and angrier came my brother's cry,
And all my soul was quivering fear, when lo!
Upon the imperilled line, suspended high,

A silver perch! My guilt that won the prey,
Now turned to merit, had a guerdon rich
Of hugs and praises, and made merry play,
Until my triumph reached its highest pitch

When all at home were told the wondrous feat,
And how the little sister had fished well.
In secret, though my fortune tasted sweet,
I wondered why this happiness befell.

    'The little lass had luck,' the gardener said:
    And so I learned, luck was with glory wed.

9

We had the self-same world enlarged for each
By loving difference of girl and boy:
The fruit that hung on high beyond my reach
He plucked for me, and oft he must employ

A measuring glance to guide my tiny shoe
Where lay firm stepping-stones, or call to mind
'This thing I like my sister may not do,
For she is little, and I must be kind.'

Thus boyish Will the nobler mastery learned
Where inward vision over impulse reigns,
Widening its life with separate life discerned,
A Like unlike, a Self that self restrains.

　　His years with others must the sweeter be
　　For those brief days he spent in loving me.

10

His sorrow was my sorrow, and his joy
Sent little leaps and laughs through all my frame;
My doll seemed lifeless and no girlish toy
Had any reason when my brother came.

I knelt with him at marbles, marked his fling
Cut the ringed stem and make the apple drop,
Or watched him winding close the spiral string
That looped the orbits of the humming top.

Grasped by such fellowship my vagrant thought
Ceased with dream-fruit dream-wishes to fulfil;
My aëry-picturing fantasy was taught
Subjection to the harder, truer skill

　　That seeks with deeds to grave a thought-tracked line,
　　And by 'What is,' 'What will be' to define.

11

School parted us; we never found again
That childish world where our two spirits mingled
Like scents from varying roses that remain
One sweetness, nor can evermore be singled.

Yet the twin habit of that early time
Lingered for long about the heart and tongue:
We had been natives of one happy clime,
And its dear accent to our utterance clung.

Till the dire years whose awful name is Change
Had grasped our souls still yearning in divorce,
And pitiless shaped them in two forms that range
Two elements which sever their life's course.

    But were another childhood-world my share,
    I would be born a little sister there

GEORGE ELIOT

8

THE PASSING
OF TIME

Beauty, sweet Love

Beauty, sweet Love, is like the morning dew
Whose short refresh upon the tender green
Cheers for a time, but till the sun doth shew
And straight 'tis gone as it had never been.
Soon doth it fade that makes the fairest flourish,
Short is the glory of the blushing rose,
The hue which thou so carefully dost nourish,
Yet which at length thou must be forced to lose.
When thou, surcharged with burthen of thy years,
Shalt bend thy wrinkles homeward to the earth,
And that, in beauty's lease expired, appears
The date of age, the Kalends of our death –
    But ah, no more! this must not be foretold,
    For women grieve to think they must be old.

SAMUEL DANIEL

Sonnet 2

When forty winters shall besiege thy brow,
And dig deep trenches in thy beauty's field,
Thy youth's proud livery, so gaz'd on now,
Will be a totter'd weed of small worth held:
Then being ask'd where all thy beauty lies,
Where all the treasure of thy lusty days,
To say within thine own deep sunken eyes
Were an all-eating shame, and thriftless praise.
How much more praise deserv'd thy beauty's use
If thou couldst answer: 'This fair child of mine
Shall sum my count, and make my old excuse', –
Proving his beauty by succession thine!
    This were to be new made when thou art old,
    And see thy blood warm when thou feel'st it cold.

WILLIAM SHAKESPEARE

Sonnet 12

When I do count the clock that tells the time,
And see the brave day sunk in hideous night;
When I behold the violet past prime,
And sable curls all silver'd o'er with white;
When lofty trees I see barren of leaves,
Which erst from heat did canopy the herd,
And summer's green all girded up in sheaves,
Borne on the bier with white and bristly beard,
Then of thy beauty do I question make,
That thou among the wastes of time must go,
Since sweets and beauties do themselves forsake
And die as fast as they see others grow;
　　And nothing 'gainst Time's scythe can make defence
　　Save breed, to brave him when he takes thee hence.

WILLIAM SHAKESPEARE

Sonnet 15

When I consider every thing that grows
Holds in perfection but a little moment,
That this huge stage presenteth nought but shows
Whereon the stars in secret influence comment;
When I perceive that men as plants increase,
Cheerèd and check'd even by the self-same sky,
Vaunt in their youthful sap, at height decrease,
And wear their brave state out of memory;
Then the conceit of this inconstant stay
Sets you most rich in youth before my sight,
Where wasteful Time debateth with Decay,
To change your day of youth to sullied night;
　　And all in war with Time for love of you,
　　As he takes from you, I engraft you new.

WILLIAM SHAKESPEARE

Sonnet 63

That time of year thou mayst in me behold
When yellow leaves, or none, or few, do hang
Upon those boughs which shake against the cold,
Bare ruin'd choirs, where late the sweet birds sang.
In me thou see'st the twilight of such day
As after sunset fadeth in the west;
Which by and by black night doth take away,
Death's second self, that seals up all in rest.
In me thou see'st the glowing of such fire,
That on the ashes of his youth doth lie,
As the death-bed whereon it must expire,
Consumed with that which it was nourish'd by.
   This thou perceivest, which makes thy love more strong,
   To love that well which thou must leave ere long.

WILLIAM SHAKESPEARE

Sonnet 104

To me, fair friend, you never can be old,
For as you were when first your eye I eyed,
Such seems your beauty still. Three winters cold
Have from the forests shook three summers' pride,
Three beauteous springs to yellow autumn turn'd
In process of the seasons have I seen,
Three April perfumes in three hot Junes burn'd,
Since first I saw you fresh, which yet are green.
Ah, yet doth beauty, like a dial-hand,
Steal from his figure, and no pace perceived;
So your sweet hue, which methinks still doth stand,
Hath motion, and mine eye may be deceived:
   For fear of which, hear this, thou age unbred;
   Ere you were born was beauty's summer dead.

WILLIAM SHAKESPEARE

Sonnet on his Being Arrived
at the Age of Twenty-Three

How soon hath Time, the subtle thief of youth,
   Stolen on his wing my three-and-twenti'th year!
   My hasting days fly on with full career,
   But my late spring no bud or blossom shew'th.

Perhaps my semblance might deceive the truth,
   That I to manhood am arrived so near,
   And inward ripeness doth much less appear,
   That some more timely-happy spirits endu'th.

Yet be it less or more, or soon or slow,
   It shall be still in strictest measure even
   To that same lot, however mean or high,

Toward which Time leads me, and the will of Heaven;
   All is, if I have grace to use it so,
   As ever in my great Task-Master's eye.

JOHN MILTON

Sonnet to the River Loddon

Ah! what a weary race my feet have run,
Since first I trod thy banks with alders crowned,
And thought my way was all through fairy ground,
Beneath thy azure sky and golden sun,
Where first my Muse to lisp her notes begun.
While pensive memory traces back the round,
Which fills the varied interval between,
Much pleasure, more of sorrow, mark the scene.
Sweet native stream, those skies and suns so pure
No more return to cheer my evening road.
Yet still one joy remains; that not obscure
Nor useless all my vacant days have flowed,
From youth's gay dawn to manhood's prime mature,
Nor with the Muse's laurel unbestowed.

THOMAS WARTON THE YOUNGER

Long time a child, and still a child, when years . . .

Long time a child, and still a child, when years
Had painted manhood on my cheek, was I, –
For yet I lived like one not born to die;
A thriftless prodigal of smiles and tears,
No hope I needed, and I knew no fears.
But sleep, though sweet, is only sleep, and waking.
I waked to sleep no more, at once o'ertaking
The vanguard of my age, with all arrears
Of duty on my back, Nor child, nor man,
Nor youth, nor sage, I find my head is grey,
For I have lost the race I never ran:
A rathe December blights my lagging May;
And still I am a child, tho' I be old,
Time is my debtor for my years untold.

HARTLEY COLERIDGE

Ozymandias

I met a traveller from an antique land
Who said: Two vast and trunkless legs of stone
Stand in the desert. Near them, on the sand,
Half sunk, a shattered visage lies, whose frown,
And wrinkled lip, and sneer of cold command
Tell that its sculptor well those passions read
Which yet survive (stamped on these lifeless things)
The hand that mocked them and the heart that fed:
And on the pedestal these words appear:
'My name is Ozymandias, King of Kings:
Look on my works, ye Mighty, and despair!'
Nothing beside remains. Round the decay
Of that colossal wreck, boundless and bare
The lone and level sands stretch far away.

PERCY BYSSHE SHELLEY

Youth and Age

O give me back the days when loose and free
  To my blind passion were the curb and rein,
  O give me back the angelic face again,
  With which all virtue buried seems to be!
O give my panting footsteps back to me,
  That are in age so slow and fraught with pain,
  And fire and moisture in the heart and brain,
  If thou wouldst have me burn and weep for thee!
If it be true thou livest alone, Amor,
  On the sweet-bitter tears of human hearts,
  In an old man thou canst not wake desire;
Souls that have almost reached the other shore
  Of a diviner love should feel the darts,
  And be as tinder to a holier fire.

HENRY LONGFELLOW

Past and Present

On four-horse coach, whose luggage pierced the sky,
  Perch'd on back seat, like clerk on office-stool,
  While wintry winds my dangling heels kept cool,
  In Whitney white envelop'd and blue tie,
Unpillow'd slumber from my half-closed eye
  Scared by the shrill tin horn; when welcome Yule
  Brought holiday season, it was thus from school
  I homeward came some forty years gone by.
Thus two long days and one long night I rode,
  Stage after stage, till the last change of team
  Stopp'd, splash'd and panting, at my sire's abode.
How nowaday from school comes home my son?
  Through duct and tunnel by a puff of steam,
  Shot like a pellet from his own pop-gun.

R. E. EGERTON WARBURTON

To a Lady seen for a few moments at Vauxhall

Time's sea hath been five years at its slow ebb,
    Long hours have to and fro let creep the sand,
Since I was tangled in thy beauty's web
    And snared by the ungloving of thine hand.
And yet I never look on midnight sky
    But I behold thine eyes' well-memory'd light;
I cannot look upon the rose's dye
    But to thy cheek my soul doth take its flight;
I cannot look on any budding flower
    But my fond ear, in fancy at thy lips
And hearkening for a love-sound, doth devour
    Its sweets in the wrong sense. Thou dost eclipse
Every delight with sweet remembering,
And grief unto my darling joys dost bring.

JOHN KEATS

Sonnet

Sweets to the sweet – farewell.   HAMLET

Time was I liked a cheesecake well enough –
    All human children have a sweetish taste;
I used to revel in a pie, or puff,
    Or tart – we all were *Tartars* in our youth;
To meet with jam or jelly was good luck,
    All candies most complacently I crumped,
A stick of liquorice was good to suck,
    And sugar was as often liked as lumped!
On treacle's 'linkèd sweetness long drawn out,'
    Or honey I could feast like any fly;
I thrilled when lollipops were hawked about;
    How pleased to compass hard-bake or bull's-eye;
How charmed if Fortune in my power cast
    Elecampane – but that campaign is past.

THOMAS HOOD

On Seeing a Little Child Spin a
Coin of Alexander the Great

This is the face of him, whose quick resource
Of eye and hand subdued Bucephalus,
And made the shadow of a startled horse
A foreground for his glory. It is thus
They hand him down; this coin of Philip's son
Recalls his life, his glories, and misdeeds;
And that abortive court of Babylon,
Where the world's throne was left among the reeds.
His dust is lost among the ancient dead,
A coin his only presence: he is gone:
And all but this half mythic image fled –
A simple child may do him shame and slight;
'Twixt thumb and finger take the golden head,
And spin the horns of Ammon out of sight.

CHARLES TURNER

A Church Romance

She turned in the high pew, until her sight
Swept the west gallery, and caught its row
Of music-men with viol book, and bow
Against the sinking sad tower-window light.

She turned again; and in her pride's despite
One strenuous viol's inspirer seemed to throw
A message from his string to her below,
Which said: 'I claim thee as my own forthright!'

Thus their hearts' bond began, in due time signed.
And long years thence, when Age had scared Romance,
At some old attitude of his or glance
That gallery-scene would break upon her mind,
With him as minstrel, ardent, young, and trim,
Bowing 'New Sabbath' or 'Mount Ephraïm'.

THOMAS HARDY

Sweet is your antique body

Sweet is your antique body, not yet young.
Beauty withheld from youth that looks for youth.
Fair only for your father. Dear among
Masters in art. To all men else uncouth
Save me; who know your smile comes very old,
Learnt of the happy dead that laughed with gods;
For earlier suns than ours have lent you gold,
Sly fauns and trees have given you jigs and nods.

But soon your heart, hot-beating like a bird's,
Shall slow down. Youth shall lop your hair,
And you must learn wry meanings in our words.
Your smile shall dull, because too keen aware;
And when for hopes your hand shall be uncurled,
Your eyes shall close, being opened to the world.

WILFRED OWEN

When I hear laughter

When I hear laughter from a tavern door,
   When I see crowds agape and in the rain
Watching on tiptoe and with stifled roar
   To see a rocket fired or a bull slain,
When misers handle gold, when orators
   Touch strong men's hearts with glory till they weep,
When cities deck their streets for barren wars
   Which have laid waste their youth, and when I keep
Calmly the count of my own life and see
   On what poor stuff my manhood's dreams were fed
Till I too learned what dole of vanity
   Will serve a human soul for daily bread,
   – Then I remember that I once was young
And lived with Esther the world's gods among.

WILFRID SCAWEN BLUNT

Dunster Church

Through the high arches dusty sunbeams stream
Gilding a bluff Elizabethan sire,
Luttrell of Somerset, whose marble dream
Marks the last winter-bed of man's desire.
Who, looking on these acquiescent hands,
Can guess the dumb hope unfulfilled, or know
What tides of spring, what green and summer lands,
Warmed the quick heart three centuries ago?

Who will remember, ninety years from now,
This August day, the heather on the hill,
Thatch in the sun . . . rich clematis . . . or how
Your seeking mind calls and mine answers still –
    And all this mortal ache, burned through to be
    An eyelid's flicker in eternity?

MARGARET WILLY

February Afternoon

Men heard this roar of parleying starlings, saw,
    A thousand years ago even as now,
    Black rooks with white gulls following the plough
So that the first are last until a caw
Commands that last are first again, – a law
    Which was of old when one, like me, dreamed how
    A thousand years might dust lie on his brow
Yet thus would birds do between hedge and shaw.

Time swims before me, making as a day
    A thousand years, while the broad ploughland oak
    Roars mill-like and men strike and bear the stroke
    Of war as ever, audacious or resigned,
And God still sits aloft in the array
    That we have wrought him, stone-deaf and stone-blind.

EDWARD THOMAS

9
THE SPIRIT
OF PLACE

Upon Westminster Bridge

Earth has not anything to show more fair:
Dull would he be of soul who could pass by
   A sight so touching in its majesty:
This City now doth, like a garment, wear
The beauty of the morning; silent, bare,
    Ships, towers, domes, theatres, and temples lie
    Open unto the fields, and to the sky;
All bright and glittering in the smokeless air.

Never did sun more beautifully steep
   In his first splendour, valley, rock, or hill;
Ne'er saw I, never felt, a calm so deep!
   The river glideth at his own sweet will:
Dear God! the very houses seem asleep;
   And all that mighty heart is lying still!

WILLIAM WORDSWORTH

On the Extinction of the Venetian Republic

Once did She hold the gorgeous East in fee,
   And was the safeguard of the West; the worth
   Of Venice did not fall below her birth,
Venice, the eldest child of liberty.

She was a maiden city, bright and free;
   No guile seduced, no force could violate;
   And when she took unto herself a mate,
She must espouse the everlasting Sea.

And what if she had seen those glories fade,
   Those titles vanish, and that strength decay, –
Yet shall some tribute of regret be paid
When her long life hath reach'd its final day:
Men are we, and must grieve when even the shade
   Of that which once was great is pass'd away.

                                   WILLIAM WORDSWORTH

Within King's College Chapel, Cambridge

Tax not the royal Saint with vain expense,
  With ill-match'd aims the Architect who plann'd
  (Albeit labouring for a scanty band
Of white-robed Scholars only) this immense

And glorious work of fine intelligence!
  Give all thou canst; high Heaven rejects the lore
  Of nicely-calculated less or more:
So deem'd the man who fashion'd for the sense

These lofty pillars, spread that branching roof
  Self-poised, and scoop'd into ten thousand cells,
  Where light and shade repose, where music dwells

  Lingering – and wandering on as loth to die;
Like thoughts whose very sweetness yieldeth proof
  That they were born for immortality.

WILLIAM WORDSWORTH

On the Castle of Chillon

Eternal Spirit of the chainless Mind!
  Brightest in dungeons, Liberty, thou art –
  For there thy habitation is the heart –
The heart which love of Thee alone can bind;

And when thy sons to fetters are consign'd,
  To fetters, and the damp vault's dayless gloom,
  Their country conquers with their martyrdom,
And Freedom's fame finds wings on every wind.

Chillon! thy prison is a holy place
  And thy sad floor an altar, for 'twas trod,
Until his very steps have left a trace
  Worn, as if thy cold pavement were a sod,
By Bonnivard! May none those marks efface!
  For they appeal from tyranny to God.

LORD BYRON

To the Nile

It flows through old hush'd Ægypt and its sands,
Like some grave mighty thought threading a dream;
And times and things, as in that vision, seem
Keeping along it their eternal stands, –
Caves, pillars, pyramids, the shepherd bands
That roam'd through the young world, the glory extreme
Of high Sesostris, and that southern beam,
The laughing queen that caught the world's great hands.
Then comes a mightier silence, stern and strong,
As of a world left empty of its throng,
And the void weighs on us; and then we wake,
And hear the fruitful stream lapsing along
'Twixt villages, and think how we shall take
Our own calm journey on for human sake.

JAMES LEIGH HUNT

A Crocodile

Hard by the lilled Nile I saw
A duskish river dragon stretched along.
The brown habergeon of his limbs enamelled
With sanguine alamandines and rainy pearl:
And on his back there lay a young one sleeping,
No bigger than a mouse; with eyes like beads,
And a small fragment of its speckled egg
Remaining on its harmless, pulpy snout;
A thing to laugh at, as it gaped to catch
The baulking merry flies. In the iron jaws
Of the great devil-beast, like a pale soul
Fluttering in rocky hell, lightsomely flew
A snowy trochilus, with roseate beak
Tearing the hairy leeches from his throat.

THOMAS LOVELL BEDDOES

In the Old Theatre, Fiesole

I traced the Circus whose gray stones incline
Where Rome and dim Etruria interjoin,
Till came a child who showed an ancient coin
That bore the image of a Constantine.

She lightly passed; nor did she once opine
How, better than all books, she had raised for me
In swift perspective Europe's history
Through the vast years of Caesar's sceptred line.

For in my distant plot of English loam
'Twas but to delve, and straightway there to find
Coins of like impress. As with one half blind
Whom common simples cure, her act flashed home
In that mute moment to my opened mind
The power, the pride, the reach of perished Rome.

THOMAS HARDY

The Oasis of Sidi Khaled

How the earth burns! Each pebble underfoot
Is as a living thing with power to wound.
The white sand quivers, and the footfall mute
Of the slow camels strikes but gives no sound,
As though they walked on flame, not solid ground.
'Tis noon, and the beasts' shadows even have fled
Back to their feet, and there is fire around
And fire beneath, and overhead the sun.
Pitiful heaven! What is this we view?
Tall trees, a river, pools, where swallows fly,
Thickets of oleander where doves coo,
Shades, deep as midnight, greenness for tired eyes.
Hark, how the light winds in the palm-tops sigh.
Oh this is rest. Oh this is paradise.

WILFRID SCAWEN BLUNT

Manchester by Night

O'er this huge town, rife with intestine wars,
Whence as from monstrous sacrificial shrines
Pillars of smoke climb heavenward, Night inclines
Black brows majestical with glimmering stars.
Her dewy silence soothes life's angry jars:
And like a mother's wan white face, who pines
Above her children's turbulent ways, so shines
The moon athwart the narrow cloudy bars.

Now toiling multitudes that hustling crush
Each other in the fateful strife for breath,
And, hounded on by divers hungers, rush
Across the prostrate ones that groan beneath,
Are swathed within the universal hush,
As life exchanges semblances with death.

MATHILDE BLIND

The Artist on Penmaenmawr

That first September day was blue and warm,
Flushing the shaly flanks of Penmaenmawr;
While youths and maidens, in the lucid calm
Exulting, bathed or bask'd from hour to hour;
What colour-passion did the artist feel!
While evermore the jarring trains went by,
Now, as for evermore, in fancy's eye,
Smutch'd with the cruel fires of Abergele;
Then fell the dark o'er the great crags and downs,
And all the night-struck mountain seem'd to say,
'Farewell! these happy skies, this peerless day!
And these fair seas – and fairer still than they,
The white-arm'd girls in dark blue bathing-gowns,
Among the snowy gulls and summer spray.'

CHARLES TENNYSON TURNER

The New Colossus

Not like the brazen giant of Greek fame,
With conquering limbs astride from land to land;
Here at our sea-washed, sunset gates shall stand
A mighty woman with a torch, whose flame
Is the imprisoned lightning, and her name
Mother of Exiles. From her beacon-hand
Glows world-wide welcome; her mild eyes command
The air-bridged harbour that twin cities frame.
'Keep, ancient lands, your storied pomp!' cries she
With silent lips. 'Give me your tired, your poor,
Your huddled masses yearning to breathe free,
The wretched refuse of your teeming shore.
Send these, the homeless, tempest-tost to me,
I lift my lamp beside the golden door!'

EMMA LAZARUS

Through American eyes

The English love their country with a love
    Steady, and simple, wordless, dignified;
I think it sets their patriotism above
    All others. We Americans have pride –
We glory in our country's short romance.
    We boast of it and love it. Frenchmen when
The ultimate menace comes, will die for France
    Logically as they lived. But Englishmen
Will serve day after day, obey the law,
    And do dull tasks that keep a nation strong.
Once I remember in London how I saw
    Pale shabby people standing in a long
Line in the twilight and the misty rain
To pay their tax. I then saw England plain.

ALICE DUER MILLER

10

WAR

On the Late Massacre in Piedmont

Avenge, O Lord, thy slaughtered saints, whose bones
    Lie scattered on the Alpine mountains cold,
    Even them who kept thy truth so pure of old
    When all our fathers worshipped stocks and stones,
Forget not; in thy book record their groans
    Who were thy sheep, and in their ancient fold
    Slain by the bloody Piedmontese that rolled
    Mother with infant down the rocks. Their moans
The vales redoubled to the hills, and they
    To heaven. Their martyred blood and ashes sow
    O'er all the Italian fields, where still doth sway
The triple tyrant, that from these may grow
    A hundredfold, who, having learnt thy way,
        Early may fly the Babylonian woe.

JOHN MILTON

Prolonged Sonnet: When the Troops were returning from Milan

From the Italian of Niccolo Degli Albizzi

If you could see, fair brother, how dead beat
   The fellows look who come through Rome today, –
   Black yellow smoke-dried visages,– you'd say
They thought their haste at going all too fleet.
Their empty victual-waggons up the street
   Over the bridge dreadfully sound and sway;
   Their eyes, as hang'd men's, turning the wrong way;
And nothing on their backs, or heads, or feet.
One sees the ribs and all the skeletons
   Of their gaunt horses; and a sorry sight
Are the torn saddles, cramm'd with straw and stones.
   They are ashamed, and march throughout the night;
Stumbling, for hunger, on their marrowbones;
   Like barrels rolling, jolting, in this plight.
Their arms all gone, not even their swords are saved;
   And each as silent as a man being shaved.

DANTE GABRIEL ROSSETTI

To the Lord General Cromwell
May 1652

Cromwell, our chief of men, who through a cloud
    Not of war only, but detractions rude,
    Guided by faith and matchless fortitude,
    To peace and truth thy glorious way hast ploughed,

And on the neck of crownèd Fortune proud
    Hast reared God's trophies, and his work pursued,
    While Darwen stream, with blood of Scots imbrued,
    And Dunbar field, resounds thy praises loud,

And Worcester's laureate wreath: yet much remains
    To conquer still; Peace hath her victories
    No less renowned than War: new foes arise,

Threatening to bind our souls with secular chains.
    Help us to save free conscience from the paw
    Of hireling wolves, whose Gospel is their maw.

JOHN MILTON

The Soldier

Yes. Whý do we áll, seeing of a soldier, bless him? bless
Our redcoats, our tars? Both these being, the greater
        part,
But frail clay, nay but foul clay. Here it is: the heart,
Since, proud, it calls the calling manly, gives a guess
That, hopes that, makesbelieve, the men must be no less;
It fancies, feigns, deems, dears the artist after his art;
And fain will find as sterling all as all is smart,
And scarlet wear the spirit of wár thére express.

Mark Christ our King. He knows war, served this
        soldiering through;
He of all can reeve a rope best. There he bides in bliss
Now, and séeing somewhére some mán do all that man
        can do,
For love he leans forth, needs his neck must fall on, kiss,
And cry 'O Christ-done deed! So God-made-flesh does
        too:
Were I come o'er again' cries Christ 'it should be this'.

                                    GERARD MANLEY HOPKINS

Peace

Now God be thanked Who has matched us with His hour,
  And caught our youth, and wakened us from sleeping,
With hand made sure, clear eye, and sharpened power,
  To turn, as swimmers into cleanness leaping,
Glad from a world grown old and cold and weary,
  Leave the sick hearts that honour could not move,
And half-men, and their dirty songs and dreary,
  And all the little emptiness of love!

Oh! we, who have known shame, we have found release there,
  Where there's no ill, no grief, but sleep has mending,
    Naught broken save this body, lost but breath;
Nothing to shake the laughing heart's long peace there
  But only agony, and that has ending;
    And the worst friend and enemy is but Death.

RUPERT BROOKE

The Dead

These hearts were woven of human joys and cares,
  Washed marvellously with sorrow, swift to mirth.
The years had given them kindness. Dawn was theirs,
  And sunset, and the colours of the earth.
These had seen movement, and heard music; known
  Slumber and waking; loved; gone proudly friended;
Felt the quick stir of wonder; sat alone;
  Touched flowers and furs and cheeks. All this is ended.

There are waters blown by changing winds to laughter
And lit by the rich skies, all day. And after,
  Frost, with a gesture, stays the waves that dance
And wandering loveliness. He leaves a white
  Unbroken glory, a gathered radiance,
A width, a shining peace, under the night.

RUPERT BROOKE

1914

War broke: and now the Winter of the world
With perishing great darkness closes in.
The foul tornado, centred at Berlin,
Is over all the width of Europe whirled,
Rending the sails of progress. Rent or furled
Are all Art's ensigns. Verse wails. Now begin
Famines of thought and feeling. Love's wine's thin.
The grain of human Autumn rots, down-hurled.

For after Spring had bloomed in early Greece,
And Summer blazed her glory out with Rome,
An Autumn softly fell, a harvest home,
A slow grand age, and rich with all increase.
But now, for us, wild Winter, and the need
Of sowings for new Spring, and blood for seed.

WILFRED OWEN

To the Prussians of England

When I remember plain heroic strength
And shining virtue shown by Ypres pools,
Then read the blither written by knaves for fools
In praise of English soldiers lying at length,
Who purely dream what England shall be made
Gloriously new, free of the old stains
By us, who pay the price that must be paid,
Will freeze all winter over Ypres plains.
Our silly dreams of peace you put aside
And brotherhood of man, for you will see
An armed mistress, braggart of the tide,
Her children slaves, under your mastery.
We'll have a word there too, and forge a knife,
Will cut the cancer threatens England's life.

IVOR GURNEY

April 1918

You, whose forebodings have been all fulfilled,
You who have heard the bell, seen the boy stand
Holding the flimsy message in his hand
While through your heart the fiery question thrilled
'Wounded or killed, which, which?' – and it was 'Killed – '
And in a kind of trance have read it, numb
But conscious that the dreaded hour was come,
No dream this dream wherewith your blood was chilled –
Oh brothers in calamity, unknown
Companions in the order of black loss,
Lift up your hearts, for you are not alone,
And let our sombre hosts together bring
Their sorrows to the shadow of the Cross
And learn the fellowship of suffering.

H. C. BRADBY

To England – A Note

I watched the boys of England where they went
Through mud and water to do appointed things.
See one a stake, and one wire-netting brings,
And one comes slowly under a burden bent
Of ammunition. Though the strength be spent
They 'carry on' under the shadowing wings
Of Death the ever-present. And hark, one sings
Although no joy from the grey skies be lent.

Are these the heroes – these? have kept from you
The power of primal savagery so long?
Shall break the devil's legions? These they are
Who do in silence what they might boast to do;
In the height of battle tell the world in song
How they do hate and fear the face of War.

IVOR GURNEY

In Hospital

Under the shadow of a hawthorn brake,
   Where bluebells draw the sky down to the wood,
Where, 'mid brown leaves, the primroses awake
   And hidden violets smell of solitude;
Beneath green leaves bright-fluttered by the wing
Of fleeting, beautiful, immortal Spring,
I should have said, 'I love you,' and your eyes
Have said, 'I, too . . .' The gods saw otherwise.

For this is winter, and the London streets
   Are full of soldiers from that far, fierce fray
Where life knows death, and where poor glory meets
   Full-face with shame, and weeps and turns away.
And in the broken, trampled foreign wood
Is horror, and the terrible scent of blood,
And love shines tremulous, like a drowning star,
Under the shadow of the wings of war.

E. NESBIT

Anthem for Doomed Youth

What passing-bells for these who die as cattle?
– Only the monstrous anger of the guns.
Only the stuttering rifles' rapid rattle
Can patter out their hasty orisons.
No mockeries now for them; no prayers nor bells;
Nor any voice of mourning save the choirs, –
The shrill, demented choirs of wailing shells;
And bugles calling for them from sad shires.

What candles may be held to speed them all?
Not in the hands of boys but in their eyes
Shall shine the holy glimmers of goodbyes.
The pallor of girls' brows shall be their pall;
Their flowers the tenderness of patient minds,
And each slow dusk a drawing-down of blinds.

WILFRED OWEN

The Next War

War's a joke for me and you,
While we know such dreams are true.

SIEGFRIED SASSOON

Out there, we walked quite friendly up to Death, –
  Sat down and ate beside him, cool and bland, –
  Pardoned his spilling mess-tins in our hand.
We've sniffed the green thick odour of his breath, –
Our eyes wept, but our courage didn't writhe.
  He's spat at us with bullets, and he's coughed
  Shrapnel. We chorused if he sang aloft,
We whistled while he shaved us with his scythe.

Oh, Death was never enemy of ours!
  We laughed at him, we leagued with him, old chum.
No soldier's paid to kick against His powers.
  We laughed, – knowing that better men would come,
And greater wars: when every fighter brags
He fights on Death, for lives; not men, for flags.

WILFRED OWEN

When you see millions of the mouthless dead

When you see millions of the mouthless dead
Across your dreams in pale battalions go,
Say not soft things as other men have said,
That you'll remember. For you need not so.
Give them not praise. For, deaf, how should they know
It is not curses heaped on each gashed head?
Nor tears. Their blind eyes see not your tears flow.
Nor honour. It is easy to be dead.
Say only this, 'They are dead.' Then add thereto,
'Yet many a better one has died before.'
Then, scanning all the o'ercrowded mass, should you
Perceive one face that you loved heretofore,
It is a spook. None wears the face you knew.
Great death has made all his for evermore.

CHARLES SORLEY

On Seeing a Piece of Our Heavy Artillery Brought into Action

Be slowly lifted up, thou long black arm,
Great Gun towering towards Heaven, about to curse;
Sway steep against them, and for years rehearse
Huge imprecations like a blasting charm!
Reach at that Arrogance which needs thy harm,
And beat it down before its sins grow worse.
Spend our resentment, cannon, – yea, disburse
Our gold in shapes of flame, our breaths in storm.

Yet, for men's sakes whom thy vast malison
Must wither innocent of enmity,
Be not withdrawn, dark arm, thy spoilure done,
Safe to the bosom of our prosperity.
But when thy spell be cast complete and whole,
May God curse thee, and cut thee from our soul!

WILFRED OWEN

The Soldier

If I should die, think only this of me:
   That there's some corner of a foreign field
That is for ever England. There shall be
   In that rich earth a richer dust concealed;
A dust whom England bore, shaped, made aware,
   Gave, once, her flowers to love, her ways to roam,
A body of England's, breathing English air,
   Washed by the rivers, blest by suns of home.

And think, this heart, all evil shed away,
   A pulse in the eternal mind, no less
     Gives somewhere back the thoughts by
       England given;
Her sights and sounds; dreams happy as her day;
   And laughter, learnt of friends; and gentleness,
     In hearts at peace, under an English heaven.

RUPERT BROOKE

The Mother

Written after reading Rupert Brooke's sonnet, 'The Soldier':

If you should die, think only this of me
In that still quietness where is space for thought,
Where parting, loss and bloodshed shall not be,
And men may rest themselves and dream of nought:
That in some place a mystic mile away
One whom you loved has drained the bitter cup
Till there is nought to drink; has faced the day
Once more, and now, has raised the standard up.

And think, my son, with eyes grown clear and dry
She lives as though for ever in your sight,
Loving the things *you* loved, with heart aglow
For country, honour, truth, traditions high,
 – Proud that you paid their price. (And if some night
Her heart should break – well, lad, you will not know.)

MAY HERSCHEL-CLARKE

The End

After the blast of lightning from the east,
The flourish of loud clouds, the Chariot Throne;
After the drums of time have rolled and ceased,
And by the bronze west long retreat is blown,

Shall Life renew these bodies? Of a truth
All death will he annul, all tears assuage? –
Or fill these void veins full again with youth,
And wash, with an immortal water, Age?

When I do ask white Age he saith not so:
'My head hangs weighed with snow.'
And when I hearken to the Earth, she saith:
'My fiery heart shrinks, aching. It is death.
Mine ancient scars shall not be glorified,
Nor my titanic tears, the seas, be dried.'

WILFRED OWEN

High Flight

Oh! I have slipped the surly bonds of earth
And danced the skies on laughter-silvered wings;
Sunward I've climbed, and joined the tumbling mirth
Of sun-split clouds – and done a hundred things
You have not dreamed of – wheeled and soared and swung
High in the sunlit silence. Hovering there,
I've chased the shouting wind along, and flung
My eager craft through footless halls of air.
Up, up the long, delirious, burning blue
I've topped the wind-swept heights with easy grace
Where never lark, nor even eagle flew.
And, while with silent, lifting mind I've trod
The high untrespassed sanctity of space,
Put out my hand, and touched the face of God.

JOHN MAGEE

11
WRITING

Loving in truth

Loving in truth, and faine in verse my love to show,
That the deare She might take some pleasure of my paine:
Pleasure might cause her reade, reading might make her know,
Knowledge might pitie winne, and pitie grace obtaine,
     I sought fit words to paint the blackest face of woe,
Studying inventions fine, her wits to entertaine:
Oft turning others' leaves, to see if thence would flow
Some fresh and fruitfull showers upon my sunne-burn'd braine.
     But words came halting forth, wanting Invention's stay,
Invention, Nature's child, fled step-dame Studie's blowes,
And others' feete still seem'd but strangers in my way.
Thus great with child to speake, and helplesse in my throwes,
     Biting my trewand pen, beating my selfe for spite,
     'Foole,' said my Muse to me, 'looke in thy heart and write.'

SIR PHILIP SIDNEY

Scorn not the Sonnet;
Critic, you have frowned

Scorn not the Sonnet; Critic, you have frowned,
Mindless of its just honours; with this key
Shakespeare unlocked his heart; the melody
Of this small lute gave ease to Petrarch's wound;
A thousand times this pipe did Tasso sound;
With it Camoëns soothed an exile's grief;
The Sonnet glittered a gay myrtle leaf
Amid the cypress with which Dante crowned
His visionary brow: a glow-worm lamp,
It cheered mild Spenser, called from Faery-land
To struggle through dark ways; and, when a damp
Fell round the path of Milton, in his hand
The Thing became a trumpet; whence he blew
Soul-animating strains – alas, too few!

WILLIAM WORDSWORTH

A Sonnet

A Sonnet is a moment's monument, –
   Memorial from the Soul's eternity
   To one dead deathless hour. Look that it be,
Whether for lustral rite or dire portent,
Of its own arduous fullness reverent:
   Carve it in ivory or in ebony,
   As Day or Night may rule; and let Time see
Its flowering crest impearled and orient.

A Sonnet is a coin: its face reveals
   The soul, – its converse, to what Power 'tis due: –
Whether for tribute in the august appeals
   Of Life, or dower in Love's high retinue,
It serve; or, 'mid the dark wharf's cavernous breath,
In Charon's palm it pay the toll to Death.

DANTE GABRIEL ROSSETTI

Nuns fret not at their convent's narrow room

Nuns fret not at their convent's narrow room;
And hermits are contented with their cells;
And students with their pensive citadels;
Maids at the wheel, the weaver at his loom,
Sit blithe and happy; bees that soar for bloom,
High as the highest Peak of Furness-fells,
Will murmur by the hour in foxglove bells;
In truth the prison, unto which we doom
Ourselves, no prison is: and hence for me,
In sundry moods, 'twas pastime to be bound
Within the Sonnet's scanty plot of ground;
Pleased if some Souls (for such there needs must be)
Who have felt the weight of too much liberty,
Should find brief solace there, as I have found.

WILLIAM WORDSWORTH

A Gulling Sonnet

The sacred muse that first made love divine
Hath made him naked and without attire;
But I will clothe him with this pen of mine,
That all the world his fashion shall admire:
His hat of hope, his band of beauty fine,
His cloak of craft, his doublet of desire,
Grief, for a girdle, shall about him twine,
His points of pride, his eyelet-holes of ire,
His hose of hate, his codpiece of conceit,
His stockings of stern strife, his shirt of shame,
His garters of vain-glory gay and slight,
His pantofles of passion will I frame;
    Pumps of presumption shall adorn his feet,
    And socks of sullenness exceeding sweet.

SIR JOHN DAVIES

On the Sonnet

If by dull rhymes our English must be chain'd,
    And, like Andromeda, the Sonnet sweet
Fetter'd, in spite of pained loveliness;
Let us find out, if we must be constrain'd,
    Sandals more interwoven and complete
To fit the naked foot of poesy;
Let us inspect the lyre, and weigh the stress
Of every chord, and see what may be gain'd
    By ear industrious, and attention meet;
Misers of sound and syllable, no less
Than Midas of his coinage, let us be
    Jealous of dead leaves in the bay wreath crown;
So, if we may not let the Muse be free,
    She will be bound with garlands of her own.

JOHN KEATS

Labour's Leisure

O for the feelings and the careless health
That found me toiling in the fields – the joy
I felt at eve with not a wish for wealth
When labour done and in the hedge put bye
My delving spade – I homeward used to hie
With thoughts of books I often read by stealth
Beneath the black thorn clumps at dinners hour
It urged my weary feet with eager speed
To hasten home where winter fires did shower
Scant light now felt as beautiful indeed
Where bending o'er my knees I used to read
With earnest heed all books that had the power
To give me joy in most delicious ways
And rest my spirits after weary days.

JOHN CLARE

Keen fitful gusts

Keen fitful gusts are whispering here and there
    Among the bushes, half leafless and dry;
    The stars look very cold about the sky,
And I have many miles on foot to fare;
Yet feel I little of the cool bleak air,
    Or of the dead leaves rustling drearily,
    Or of those silver lamps that burn on high,
Or of the distance from home's pleasant lair:
For I am brimful of the friendliness
    That in a little cottage I have found;
Of fair-haired Milton's eloquent distress,
    And all his love for gentle Lycid' drown'd,
Of lovely Laura in her light green dress,
    And faithful Petrarch gloriously crown'd.

JOHN KEATS

On first looking into Chapman's Homer

Much have I travell'd in the realms of gold,
    And many goodly states and kingdoms seen;
    Round many western islands have I been
Which bards in fealty to Apollo hold.
Oft of one wide expanse had I been told,
    That deep-brow'd Homer ruled as his demesne:
    Yet did I never breathe its pure serene
Till I heard Chapman speak out loud and bold:
Then felt I like some watcher of the skies
    When a new planet swims into his ken;
Or like stout Cortez when with eagle eyes
    He stared at the Pacific – and all his men
Look'd at each other with a wild surmise –
    Silent, upon a peak in Darien.

JOHN KEATS

Chaucer

An old man in a lodge within a park;
    The chamber walls depicted all around
    With portraitures of huntsman, hawk, and hound,
    And the hurt deer. He listeneth to the lark,
Whose song comes with the sunshine through the dark
    Of painted glass in leaden lattice bound;
    He listeneth and he laugheth at the sound,
    Then writeth in a book like any clerk.
He is the poet of the dawn, who wrote
    The Canterbury Tales, and his old age
    Made beautiful with song; and as I read
I hear the crowing cock, I hear the note
    Of lark and linnet, and from every page
    Rise odours of ploughed field or flowery mead.

HENRY LONGFELLOW

Oh that my heart could hit upon a strain

Oh that my heart could hit upon a strain
Would strike the music of my soul's desire;
Or that my soul could find that sacred vein
That sets the consort of the angels' choir.
Or that that spirit of especial grace
That cannot stoop beneath the state of heaven
Within my soul would take his settled place
With angels' *Ens*, to make his glory even.
Then should the name of my most gracious King,
And glorious God, in higher tunes be sounded
Of heavenly praise, than earth hath power to sing,
Where heaven, and earth, and angels, are confounded.
    And souls may sing while all heart strings are broken;
    His praise is more than can in praise be spoken.

NICHOLAS BRETON

One day I wrote her name upon the strand

One day I wrote her name upon the strand,
But Came the waves and washèd it away:
Again I wrote it with a second hand,
But came the tide, and made my pains his prey.
Vain man, said she, that dost in vain assay,
A mortal thing so to immortalise,
But I myself shall like to this decay,
And eke my name be wipèd out likewise.
Not so (quod I), let baser things devise
To die in dust, but you shall live by fame:
My verse your virtues rare shall eternise,
And in the heavens write your glorious name.
    Where whenas death shall all the world subdue,
    Our love shall live, and later life renew.

EDMUND SPENSER

How many paltry, foolish, painted things

How many paltry, foolish, painted things,
That now in coaches trouble every street,
Shall be forgotten, whom no poet sings,
Ere they be well-wrapped in their winding sheet?
Where I to thee Eternity shall give,
When nothing else remaineth of these days,
And queens hereafter shall be glad to live
Upon the alms of thy superfluous praise;
Virgins and matrons reading these my rhymes,
Shall be so much delighted with thy story,
That they shall grieve, they lived not in these times,
To have seen thee, their Sex's only glory:
    So shalt thou fly above the vulgar throng,
    Still to survive in my immortal song.

MICHAEL DRAYTON

Sonnet 18

Shall I compare thee to a summer's day?
Thou art more lovely and more temperate:
Rough winds do shake the darling buds of May,
And summer's lease hath all too short a date:
Sometime too hot the eye of heaven shines,
And often is his gold complexion dimm'd;
And every fair from fair sometime declines,
By chance or nature's changing course untrimm'd;
But thy eternal summer shall not fade,
Nor lose possession of that fair thou owest;
Nor shall Death brag thou wander'st in his shade,
When in eternal lines to time thou grow'st:
    So long as men can breathe, or eyes can see,
    So long lives this, and this gives life to thee.

WILLIAM SHAKESPEARE

Let others sing

Let others sing of knights and paladins
In agèd accents and untimely words,
Paint shadows in imaginary lines,
Which well the reach of their high wits records:
But I must sing of thee, and those fair eyes
Authentic shall my verse in time to come,
When yet the unborn shall say, 'Lo, where she lies,
Whose beauty made him speak that else was dumb.'
These are the arks, the trophies, I erect,
That fortify thy name against old age;
And these thy sacred virtues must protect
Against the dark and Time's consuming rage.
    Though the error of my youth in them appear,
    Suffice they show I lived, and loved thee dear.

SAMUEL DANIEL

To Mary Unwin

Mary! I want a lyre with other strings,
   Such aid from heaven as some have feign'd they drew,
   An eloquence scarce given to mortals, new
And undebased by praise of meaner things,

That ere through age or woe I shed my wings
   I may record thy worth with honour due,
   In verse as musical as thou art true,
Verse that immortalizes whom it sings: —

But thou hast little need. There is a Book
   By seraphs writ with beams of heavenly light,
On which the eyes of God not rarely look,
   A chronicle of actions just and bright —

There all thy deeds, my faithful Mary, shine;
And since thou own'st that praise, I spare thee mine.

WILLIAM COWPER

To a Friend, an Epigram of Him

Sir Inigo doth fear it as I hear
(And labours to seem worthy of that fear)
That I should write upon him some sharp verse,
Able to eat into his bones and pierce
The marrow! Wretch, I 'quit thee of thy pain.
Th 'art too ambitious: and dost fear in vain!
The Lybian lion hunts no butterflies,
He makes the camel and dull ass his prize.
If thou be so desirous to be read,
Seek out some hungry painter, that for bread,
With rotten chalk, or coal upon a wall,
Will well design thee, to be viewed of all
   That sit upon the common draught: or Strand!
   Thy forehead is too narrow for my brand.

BEN JONSON

To My Book

It will be looked for, book, when some but see
Thy title, *Epigrams*, and named of me,
Thou should'st be bold, licentious, full of gall,
Wormwood, and sulphur, sharp, and toothed withal;
Become a petulant thing, hurl ink, and wit,
As madmen stones: not caring whom they hit.
Deceive their malice, who could wish it so.
And by thy wiser temper, let men know
Thou are not covetous of least self-fame,
Made from the hazard of another's shame:
Much less with lewd, profane, and beastly phrase,
To catch the world's loose laughter, or vain gaze.
He that departs with his own honesty
For vulgar praise, doth it too dearly buy.

                                                        BEN JONSON

Dedication (to Leigh Hunt, Esq.)

Glory and Loveliness have passed away;
    For if we wander out in early morn,
    No wreathèd incense do we see upborne
Into the east to meet the smiling day:
No crowd of nymphs soft-voiced and young and gay,
    In woven baskets bringing ears of corn,
    Roses, and pinks, and violets, to adorn
The shrine of Flora in her early May.
But there are left delights as high as these,
    And I shall ever bless my destiny,
That in a time when under pleasant trees
    Pan is no longer sought, I feel a free,
A leafy luxury, seeing I could please,
    With these poor offerings, a man like thee.

                                                        JOHN KEATS

12

DEATH

On His Dead Wife

Methought I saw my late espousèd saint
   Brought to me like Alcestis from the grave,
   Whom Jove's great son to her glad husband gave,
   Rescued from death by force, though pale and faint.
Mine, as whom washed from spot of childbed taint
   Purification in the old Law did save,
   And such as yet once more I trust to have
   Full sight of her in heaven without restraint,
Came vested all in white, pure as her mind.
   Her face was veiled, yet to my fancied sight
   Love, sweetness, goodness, in her person shined
So clear as in no face with more delight.
   But O as to embrace me she inclined,
   I waked, she fled, and day brought back my night.

JOHN MILTON

Death

What has this bugbear Death that's worth our care?
After a life in pain and sorrow past,
After deluding hope and dire despair,
Death only gives us quiet at the last.
How strangely are our love and hate misplaced!
Freedom we seek, and yet from freedom flee;
Courting those tyrant-sins that chain us fast,
And shunning Death that only sets us free.
'Tis not a foolish fear of future pains –
Why should they fear who keep their souls from stains? –
That makes me dread thy terrors, Death, to see;
'Tis not the loss of riches or of fame,
Or the vain toys the vulgar pleasures name:
'Tis nothing, Celia, but the losing thee.

WILLIAM WALSH

On the Death of Mr Richard West

In vain to me the smiling mornings shine
And redd'ning Phoebus lifts his golden fire:
The birds in vain their amorous descant join;
Or cheerful fields resume their green attire:
These ears, alas! for other notes repine,
A different object do these eyes require:
My lonely anguish melts no heart but mine;
And in my breast the imperfect joys expire.
Yet morning smiles the busy race to cheer,
And new-born pleasure brings to happier men:
The fields to all their wonted tribute bear:
To warm their little loves the birds complain:
I fruitless mourn to him that cannot hear,
And weep the more, because I weep in vain.

THOMAS GRAY

Sonnet upon the Punishment of Death

The Roman Consul doomed his sons to die
Who had betrayed their country. The stern word
Afforded (may it through all time afford)
A theme for praise and admiration high.
Upon the surface of humanity
He rested not; its depths his mind explored;
He felt; but his parental bosom's lord
Was Duty, – Duty calmed his agony.
And some, we know, when they by wilful act
A single human life have wrongly taken,
Pass sentence on themselves, confess the fact,
And, to atone for it, with soul unshaken
Kneel at the feet of Justice, and, for faith
Broken with all mankind, solicit death.

WILLIAM WORDSWORTH

When I have fears

When I have fears that I may cease to be
    Before my pen has glean'd my teeming brain,
Before high-pilèd books, in charact'ry,
    Hold like rich garners the full-ripen'd grain;
When I behold, upon the night's starr'd face,
    Huge cloudy symbols of a high romance,
And feel that I may never live to trace
    Their shadows, with the magic hand of chance;
And when I feel, fair creature of an hour!
    That I shall never look upon thee more,
Never have relish in the faery power
    Of unreflecting love! – then on the shore
Of the wide world I stand alone, and think,
Till Love and Fame to nothingness do sink.

JOHN KEATS

A blast of wind, a momentary breath

A blast of wind, a momentary breath,
A watery bubble symbolised with air,
A sun-blown rose, but for a season fair,
A ghostly glance, a skeleton of death;
A morning dew, pearling the grass beneath,
Whose moisture sun's appearance doth impair;
A lightning glimpse, a muse of thought and care,
A planet's shot, a shade which followeth,
A voice which vanisheth so soon as heard,
The thriftless heir of time, a rolling wave,
A show, no more in action than regard,
A mass of dust, world's momentary slave,
    Is man, in state of our old Adam made,
    Soon born to die, soon flourishing to fade.

BARNABE BARNES

On Bala Hill

With many a weary step at length I gain
Thy summit, Bala! and the cool breeze plays
Cheerily round my brow – as hence the gaze
Returns to dwell upon the journey'd plain.

'Twas a long way and tedious! – to the eye
Tho' fair th'extended Vale, and fair to view
The falling leaves of many a faded hue
That eddy in the wild gust moaning by!

Ev'n so it far'd with Life! in discontent
Restless thro' Fortune's mingled scenes I went,
Yet wept to think they would return no more!
O cease fond heart! in such sad thoughts to roam,
For surely thou ere long shalt reach thy home,
And pleasant is the way that lies before.

SAMUEL TAYLOR COLERIDGE

Summer Dawn

Pray but one prayer for me 'twixt thy closed lips,
  Think but one thought of me up in the stars.
  The summer night waneth, the morning light slips
Faint and grey 'twixt the leaves of the aspen, betwixt the
    cloud-bars,
That are patiently waiting there for the dawn:
  Patient and colourless, though Heaven's gold
Waits to float through them along with the sun.
Far out in the meadows, above the young corn,
  The heavy elms wait, and restless and cold
The uneasy wind rises; the roses are dun;
Through the long twilight they pray for the dawn,
Round the lone house in the midst of the corn.
  Speak but one word to me over the corn,
  Over the tender, bowed locks of the corn.

WILLIAM MORRIS

Remember

Remember me when I am gone away,
  Gone far away into the silent land;
  When you can no more hold me by the hand
Nor I half turn to go yet turning stay.
Remember me when no more day by day
  You tell me of our future that you planned:
  Only remember me; you understand
It will be late to counsel then or pray.
Yet if you should forget me for a while
  And afterwards remember, do not grieve:
  For if the darkness and corruption leave
  A vestige of the thoughts that once I had,
Better by far you should forget and smile
  Than that you should remember and be sad.

CHRISTINA ROSSETTI

After Death

The curtains were half drawn, the floor was swept
  And strewn with rushes, rosemary and may
  Lay thick upon the bed on which I lay,
Where through the lattice ivy-shadows crept.
He leaned above me, thinking that I slept
  And could not hear him; but I heard him say:
  'Poor child, poor child:' and as he turned away
Came a deep silence, and I knew he wept.
He did not touch the shroud, or raise the fold
  That hid my face, or take my hand in his,
    Or ruffle the smooth pillows for my head:
    He did not love me living; but once dead
  He pitied me; and very sweet it is
To know he still is warm though I am cold.

CHRISTINA ROSSETTI

Hospital Barge

Budging the sluggard ripples of the Somme,
A barge round old Cérisy slowly slewed.
Softly her engines down the current screwed,
And chuckled softly with contented hum,
Till fairy tinklings struck their croonings dumb.
The waters rumpling at the stern subdued;
The lock-gate took her bulging amplitude;
Gently from out the gurgling lock she swum.

One reading by that calm bank shaded eyes
To watch her lessening westward quietly.
Then, as she neared the bend, her funnel screamed.
And that long lamentation made him wise
How unto Avalon, in agony,
Kings passed in the dark barge which Merlin dreamed.

WILFRED OWEN

The Cross of Snow

In the long, sleepless watches of the night,
    A gentle face – the face of one long dead –
    Looks at me from the wall, where round its head
    The night-lamp casts a halo of pale light.
Here in this room she died; and soul more white
    Never through martyrdom of fire was led
    To its repose; nor can in books be read
    The legend of a life more benedight.
There is a mountain in the distant West
    That, sun-defying, in its deep ravines
    Displays a cross of snow upon its side.
Such is the cross I wear upon my breast
    These eighteen years, through all the changing scenes
    And seasons, changeless since the day she died.

HENRY LONGFELLOW

Doricha
From the Greek of Poseidippos

So now the very bones of you are gone
Where they were dust and ashes long ago;
And there was the last ribbon you tied on
To bind your hair, and that is dust also;
And somewhere there is dust that was of old
A soft and scented garment that you wore –
The same that once till dawn did closely fold
You in with fair Charaxus, fair no more.

But Sappho, and the white leaves of her song,
Will make your name a word for all to learn,
And all to love thereafter, even while
It's but a name; and this will be as long
As there are distant ships that will return
Again to your Naucratis and the Nile.

EDWIN ARLINGTON ROBINSON

The Dead Poet

I dreamed of him last night, I saw his face
All radiant and unshadowed of distress,
And as of old, in music measureless,
I heard his golden voice and marked him trace
Under the common thing the hidden grace,
And conjure wonder out of emptiness,
Till mean things put on beauty like a dress
And all the world was an enchanted place.
And then methought outside a fast locked gate
I mourned the loss of unrecorded words,
Forgotten tales and mysteries half said,
Wonders that might have been articulate,
And voiceless thoughts like murdered singing birds.
And so l woke and knew that he was dead.

LORD ALFRED DOUGLAS

An Old Labourer

Here was no shivering winter, nipped and sere,
Its music muted and the sap run dry,
But the full harvest of a mellowing year
Serene beneath the late October sky.
Laden, these boughs, with fruit of toiling days:
Rough jest, an evening pipe with some staunch friend;
A lover's wonder in the fields' quiet ways
Burning still clearer here at autumn's end.

Undimmed the eyes that watched slow seasons change
From cowslip days to mist and woods aflame,
Till seventy years rolled back towards his birth;
The harvest ripe, he feared in death no strange
Dark enemy – but, calm when twilight came,
Lay down to join his old, first love, the earth.

MARGARET WILLY

Verity

In memory of Captain Hedley Verity, injured in Sicily.
Taken POW, buried at Caserta. Pre-war, Yorkshire
and England slow left-arm bowler

The ruth and truth you taught have come full circle
On that fell island all whose history lies,
Far now from Bramhall Lane and far from Scarborough
You recollect how foolish are the wise.

On this great ground more marvellous than Lord's
 — Time takes more spin than nineteen thirty four —
You face at last that vast that Bradman-shaming
Batsman whose cuts obey no natural law.

Run up again, as gravely smile as ever,
Veer without fear your left unlucky arm
In His so dark direction, but no length
However lovely can disturb the harm
That is His style, defer the winning drive
Or shake the crowd from their uproarious calm.

DRUMMOND ALLISON

13

QUESTIONS, DOUBTS, REFLECTIONS

A Great Favourite Beheaded

The bloudy trunck of him who did possesse
   Above the rest a haplesse happy state,
   This little Stone doth Seale, but not depresse,
   And scarce can stop the rowling of his fate.

Brasse Tombes which justice hath deny'd t'his fault,
   The common pity to his vertues payes,
   Adorning an Imaginary vault,
   Which from our minds time strives in vaine to raze.

Ten yeares the world upon him falsly smild,
   Sheathing in fawning lookes the deadly knife
   Long aymèd at his head; That so beguild
   It more securely might bereave his Life;

Then threw him to a Scaffold from a Throne,
Much Doctrine lyes under this little stone.

SIR RICHARD FANSHAWE

To Cyriack Skinner

Cyriack, whose grandsire, on the royal bench
   Of British Themis, with no mean applause
   Pronounced, and in his volumes taught, our laws,
Which others at their bar so often wrench;

Today deep thoughts resolve with me to drench
   In mirth, that after no repenting draws;
   Let Euclid rest, and Archimedes pause,
And what the Swede intend, and what the French.

To measure life learn thou betimes, and know
   Toward solid good what leads the nearest way;
     For other things mild Heaven a time ordains,

And disapproves that care, though wise in show,
   That with superfluous burden loads the day,
     And, when God sends a cheerful hour, refrains.

JOHN MILTON

Doth then the world go thus

Doth then the world go thus, doth all thus move?
  Is this the justice which on Earth we find?
  Is this that firm decree which all both bind?
Are these your influences, Powers above?

  Those souls which vice's moody mists most blind,
Blind Fortune, blindly, most their friend doth prove;
And they who thee, poor idol, Virtue! love.
  Ply like a feather toss'd by storm and wind.

Ah! if a Providence doth sway this all,
  Why should best minds groan under most distress?
Or why should pride humility make thrall,
  And injuries the innocent oppress?

Heavens! hinder, stop this fate; or grant a time
When good may have, as well as bad, their prime.

WILLIAM DRUMMOND

It is a beauteous

It is a beauteous evening, calm and free,
The holy time is quiet as a Nun
Breathless with adoration; the broad sun
Is sinking down in its tranquillity;
The gentleness of heaven broods o'er the Sea:
Listen! the mighty Being is awake,
And doth with his eternal motion make
A sound like thunder – everlastingly.
Dear Child! dear Girl! that walkest with me here,
If thou appear untouched by solemn thought,
Thy nature is not therefore less divine:
Thou liest in Abraham's bosom all the year;
And worshipp'st at the Temple's inner shrine,
God being with thee when we know it not.

WILLIAM WORDSWORTH

The world is too much with us

The world is too much with us; late and soon,
Getting and spending, we lay waste our powers:
Little we see in Nature that is ours;
We have given our hearts away, a sordid boon!
This Sea that bares her bosom to the moon;
The winds that will be howling at all hours,
And are up-gathered now like sleeping flowers;
For this, for everything, we are out of tune;
It moves us not. – Great God! I'd rather be
A Pagan suckled in a creed outworn;
So might l, standing on this pleasant lea,
Have glimpses that would make me less forlorn;
Have sight of Proteus rising from the sea;
Or hear old Triton blow his wreathèd horn.

WILLIAM WORDSWORTH

On the Projected Kendal and
Windermere Railway

Is then no nook of English ground secure
From rash assault? Schemes of retirement sown
In youth, and 'mid the busy world kept pure
As when their earliest flowers of hope were blown,
Must perish; – how can they this blight endure?
And must he too the ruthless change bemoan
Who scorns a false utilitarian lure
'Mid his paternal fields at random thrown?
Baffle the threat, bright Scene, from Orrest-head
Given to the passing traveller's rapturous glance:
Plead for thy peace, though beautiful romance
Of nature, and, if human hearts be dead,
Speak, passing winds; ye torrents, with your strong
And constant voice, protest against the wrong.

WILLIAM WORDSWORTH

London 1802

O Friend! I know not which way I must look
  For comfort, being, as I am, opprest
  To think that now our life is only drest
For show; mean handiwork of craftsman, cook,

Or groom! — We must run glittering like a brook
  In the open sunshine, or we are unblest;
  The wealthiest man among us is the best:
No grandeur now in Nature or in book

Delights us. Rapine, avarice, expense,
  This is idolatry; and these we adore:
  Plain living and high thinking are no more:

The homely beauty of the good old cause
Is gone; our peace, our faithful innocence,
  And pure religion breathing household laws.

WILLIAM WORDSWORTH

Milton

Milton! thou shouldst be living at this hour:
England hath need of thee: she is a fen
  Of stagnant waters: altar, sword and pen,
Fireside, the heroic wealth of hall and bower,
Have forfeited their ancient English dower
  Of inward happiness. We are selfish men;
  O raise us up, return to us again,
And give us manners, virtue, freedom, power!
Thy soul was like a Star, and dwelt apart;
  Thou hadst a voice whose sound was like the sea:
  Pure as the naked heavens, majestic, free,
  So didst thou travel on life's common way,
In cheerful godliness; and yet thy heart
  The lowliest duties on herself did lay.

WILLIAM WORDSWORTH

Why did I laugh tonight?

Why did I laugh tonight? No voice will tell:
    No God, no Demon of severe response,
Deigns to reply from Heaven or from Hell.
    Then to my human heart I turn at once.
Heart! Thou and I are here, sad and alone;
    Say, wherefore did I laugh? O mortal pain!
O Darkness! Darkness! ever must I moan,
    To question Heaven and Hell and Heart in vain.
Why did I laugh? I know this Being's lease,
    My fancy to its utmost blisses spreads;
Yet would I on this very midnight cease,
    And the world's gaudy ensigns see in shreds;
Verse, Fame, and Beauty are intense indeed,
But Death intenser – Death is Life's high meed.

                                    JOHN KEATS

Fame, like a wayward girl

Fame, like a wayward girl, will still be coy
    To those who woo her with too slavish knees,
But makes surrender to some thoughtless boy,
    And dotes the more upon a heart at ease;
She is a Gipsy will not speak to those
    Who have not learnt to be content without her;
A Jilt, whose ear was never whisper'd close,
    Who thinks they scandal her who talk about her;
A very Gipsy is she, Nilus-born,
    Sister-in-law to jealous Potiphar;
Ye love-sick Bards! repay her scorn for scorn;
    Ye Artists lovelorn! madmen that ye are!
Make your best bow to her and bid adieu,
Then, if she likes it, she will follow you.

                                    JOHN KEATS

Fancy in Nubibus

or The Poet in the Clouds

O! it is pleasant, with a heart at ease,
    Just after sunset, or by moonlight skies,
To make the shifting clouds be what you please,
    Or let the easily persuaded eyes
Own each quaint likeness issuing from the mould
    Of a friend's fancy; or with head bent low
And cheek aslant see rivers flow of gold
    'Twixt crimson banks; and then, a traveller, go
From mount to mount through Cloudland; gorgeous land!
    Or list'ning to the tide, with closèd sight,
Be that blind bard, who on the Chian strand
    By those deep sounds possessed with inward light,
Beheld the Iliad and the Odyssee
    Rise to the swelling of the voiceful sea.

SAMUEL TAYLOR COLERIDGE

Nutting

The sun had stooped his westward clouds to win
Like weary traveller seeking for an Inn
When from the hazelly wood we glad descried
The ivied gateway by the pasture side
Long had we sought for nutts amid the shade
Where silence fled the rustle which we made
When torn by briars and brushed by sedges rank
We left the wood and on the velvet bank
Of short sward pasture ground we sat us down
To shell our nutts before we reached the town
The near hand stubble field with mellow glower
Showed the dimmed blaze of poppys still in flower
And sweet the mole hills smelt we sat upon
And now the thymes in bloom but where is pleasure gone?

JOHN CLARE

Careless Rambles

I love to wander at my idle will
In summers luscious prime about the fields
And kneel when thirsty at the little rill
To sip the draught its pebbly bottom yields
And where the maple bush its fountain shields
To lie and rest a swailey hour away
And crop the swelling peascod from the land
Or mid the uplands woodland walks to stray
Where oaks for aye o'er their old shadows stand
Neath whose dark foliage with a welcome hand
I pluck the luscious strawberry ripe and red
As beautys lips – and in my fancys dreams
As mid the velvet moss I musing tread
Feel life as lovely as her picture seems.

JOHN CLARE

Hay Making

'Tis hay-time and the red complexioned sun
Was scarcely up ere Black birds had begun
Along the meadow hedges here and there
To sing loud songs to the sweet smelling air
Where breath of flowers and grass and breathing cow
Fling o'er ones senses streams of fragrance now
While in some pleasant nook the swain and maid
Lean o'er their rakes and loiter in the shade
To bend a minute o'er the bridge and throw
Crumbs from their pockets to the fish below
 – Hark at that happy shout – and song between
'Tis pleasures birthday in her meadow scene
What joy seems half so rich from rapture won
As the loud laugh of maidens in the sun?

JOHN CLARE

Silence

There is a silence where hath been no sound,
   There is a silence where no sound may be,
   In the cold grave – under the deep, deep sea,
Or in wide desert where no life is found,
Which hath been mute, and still must sleep profound
   No voice is hushed – no life treads silently,
   But clouds and cloudy shadows wander free,
That never spoke, over the idle ground.

But in green ruins, in the desolate walls
   Of antique palaces where Man hath been,
Though the dun fox or wild hyena calls,
   And owls, that flit continually between,
Shriek to the echo, and the low winds moan –
There the true Silence is, self-conscious and alone.

THOMAS HOOD

England in 1819

An old, mad, blind, despised, and dying king, –
Princes, the dregs of their dull race, who flow
Through public scorn, – mud from a muddy spring, –
Rulers who neither see, nor feel, nor know,
But leech-like to their fainting country cling,
Till they drop, blind in blood, without a blow, –
A people starved and stabbed in the untilled field, –
An army, which liberticide and prey
Makes as a two-edged sword to all who wield, –
Golden and sanguine laws which tempt and slay;
Religion Christless, Godless – a book sealed;
A Senate, – Time's worst statute unrepealed, –
Are graves, from which a glorious Phantom may
Burst, to illumine our tempestuous day.

PERCY BYSSHE SHELLEY

Think that the grass upon thy grave is green

Think that the grass upon thy grave is green;
   Think that thou seest thine own empty chair;
   The empty garments thou wast wont to wear;
   The empty room where long thy haunt hath been:
Think that the lane, the meadow, and the wood
   And mountain summit feel thy foot no more,
   Nor the loud thoroughfare, nor sounding shore:
   All mere blank space where thou thyself hast stood.
Amid this thought-created silence say
   To thy stripped soul, what am I now and where?
   Then turn and face the petty narrowing care
Which has been gnawing thee for many a day,
   And it will die as dies a wailing breeze
   Lost in the solemn roar of boundless seas.

JAMES SMETHAM

Autumn Idleness

This sunlight shames November where he grieves
  In dead red leaves, and will not let him shun
  The day, though bough with bough be over-run.
But with a blessing every glade receives
High salutation; while from hillock-eaves
  The deer gaze calling, dappled white and dun,
  As if, being foresters of old, the sun
Had marked them with the shade of forest-leaves.

Here dawn today unveiled her magic glass;
  Here noon now gives the thirst and takes the dew;
Till eve bring rest when other good things pass.
  And here the lost hours the lost hours renew
While I still lead my shadow o'er the grass,
  Nor know, for longing, that which I should do.

DANTE GABRIEL ROSSETTI

Hélas!

To drift with every passion till my soul
Is a stringed lute on which all winds can play,
Is it for this that I have given away
Mine ancient wisdom, and austere control?
Methinks my life is a twice-written scroll
Scrawled over on some boyish holiday
With idle songs for pipe and virelay,
Which do but mar the secret of the whole.
Surely there was a time I might have trod
The sunlit heights, and from life's dissonance
Struck one clear chord to reach the ears of God:
Is that time dead? lo! with a little rod
I did but touch the honey of romance –
And must I lose a soul's inheritance?

OSCAR WILDE

On the Sale by Auction of
Keats' Love Letters

These are the letters which Endymion wrote
   To one he loved in secret, and apart.
   And now the brawlers of the auction mart
Bargain and bid for each poor blotted note,
Ay! for each separate pulse of passion quote
   The merchant's price. I think they love not art
   Who break the crystal of a poet's heart
That small and sickly eyes may glare and gloat.

Is it not said that many years ago,
   In a far Eastern town, some soldiers ran
   With torches through the midnight, and began
To wrangle for mean raiment, and to throw
   Dice for the garments of a wretched man,
Not knowing the God's wonder, or His woe?

OSCAR WILDE

Fashion

See those resplendent creatures, as they glide
    O'er scarlet carpet, between footmen tall,
    From sumptuous carriage to effulgent hall –
A dazzling vision in their pomp and pride!
See that choice supper – needless – cast aside –
    Though worth a thousand fortunes, counting all,
    To them for whom no crumb of it will fall –
The starved and homeless in the street outside.

Some day the little great god will decree
    That overmuch connotes the underbred,
    That pampered body means an empty head,
And wealth displayed the last vulgarity.
When selfish greed becomes a social sin
The world's regeneration may begin.

ADA CAMBRIDGE

To —

Three rompers run together, hand in hand.
The middle boy stops short, the others hurtle:
What bumps, what shrieks, what laughter turning turtle.
Love, racing between us two, has planned
A sudden mischief: shortly he will stand
And we shall shock. We cannot help but fall;
What matter? Why, it will not hurt at all,
Our youth is supple, and the world is sand.

Better our lips should bruise our eyes, than He,
Rude Love, out-run our breath; you pant, and I,
I cannot run much farther, mind that we
Both laugh with Love; and having tumbled, try
To go forever children, hand in hand.
The sea is rising . . . and the world is sand.

WILFRED OWEN

It was upon

It was upon a July evening.
At a stile I stood, looking along a path
Over the country by a second Spring
Drenched perfect green again. 'The lattermath
Will be a fine one.' So the stranger said,
A wandering man. Albeit I stood at rest,
Flushed with desire I was. The earth outspread,
Like meadows of the future, I possessed.

And as an unaccomplished prophecy
The stranger's words, after the interval
Of a score years, when those fields are by me
Never to be recrossed, now I recall,
This July eve, and question, wondering,
What of the lattermath to this hoar Spring?

EDWARD THOMAS

INDEX OF POEM TITLES

INDEX OF FIRST LINES

To seem the stranger lies my lot, my life 93
Today I have been happy. All the day 57

Under the shadow of a hawthorn brake 138

War broke: and now the Winter of the world 136
We had the self-same world enlarged for each 105
Were I as base as is the lowly plain 4
What are we first? First, animals; and next 56
What has this bugbear Death that's worth our care? 159
What passing-bells for these who die as cattle? 139
What smouldering senses in death's sick delay 34
When forty winters shall besiege thy brow 109
When I consider every thing that grows 110
When I consider how my light is spent 70
When I do count the clock that tells the time 110
When I have fears that I may cease to be 161
When I hear laughter from a tavern door 117
When I remember plain heroic strength 136
When I was forty, and two feathers sprung 35
When I would think of you, my mind holds only 24
When men shall find thy flower, thy glory, pass 5
When our two souls stand up erect and strong 9
When they did greet me father, sudden awe 98
When you see millions of the mouthless dead 141
When you shall see me in the toils of Time 52
When you so wildly loved her, she was cold 48
Who so list to hounte I know where is an hynde 41
Why did I laugh tonight? No voice will tell 176
Why didst thou promise such a beauteous day 50
With how sad steps, ô Moone, thou climb'st the skies 43
With many a weary step at length I gain 162

Yes. Whý do we áll, seeing of a soldier, bless him? bless 134
You blessed shades, which give mee silent rest 46
You must not wonder, though you think it strange 47
You, whose forebodings have been all fulfilled 137

Distributors for the Wordsworth Poetry Library

Great Britain and Ireland
Wordsworth Editions Limited
Cumberland House
Crib Street, Ware,
Hertfordshire SG12 9ET
Telephone 01920 465 167
Fax 01920 462 267

USA, Canada and Mexico
Universal Sales & Marketing Inc
230 Fifth Avenue, Suite 1212
New York,
NY 10001, USA
Telephone 212-481-3500
Fax 212-481-3534

Portugal
International Publishing Services Ltd
Rua da Cruz da Carreira 4B
1100 Lisboa
Telephone 01-570 051
Fax 01-352 2066

Italy
Magis Books SRL
Via Raffaello 31c
Zona ind Mancasale
42100 Regio Emillia
Telephone 0522-920 999
Fax 0522-920 666

Australia and Papua New Guinea
Peribo Pty Limited
58 Beaumont Road
Mount Kuring-Gai
NSW 2080, Australia
Telephone (02)457 0011
Fax (02) 457 0022

Singapore, Malaysia & Brunei
Paul & Elizabeth Book Services Pte Ltd
163 Tanglin Road No 03-15/16
Tanglin Mall, Singapore 1024
Telephone (65) 735-7308
Fax (65) 735-9747

New Zealand
Allphy Book Distributors Limited
4–6 Charles Street, Eden Terrace
Auckland
Telephone (09) 377 3096
Fax (09) 302 2770

Southern Africa
Struik Book Distributors (Pty) Ltd
Graph Avenue,
Montague Gardens 7441
P O Box 193, Maitland 7405
South Africa
Telephone 021-551-5900
Fax 021-551-1124

The Wordsworth Poetry Library

Works of:

Matthew Arnold

William Blake

The Bronte Sisters

Rupert Brooke

Robert Browning

Elizabeth Barrett Browning

Robert Burns

Lord Byron

Geoffrey Chaucer

G. K. Chesterton

John Clare

Samuel Taylor Coleridge

Emily Dickinson

John Donne

John Dryden

Thomas Hardy

George Herbert

Gerard Manley Hopkins

A. E. Housman

James Joyce

John Keats

Rudyard Kipling

D. H. Lawrence

Henry Wadsworth Longfellow

Macaulay

Andrew Marvell

John Milton

Wilfred Owen

'Banjo' Paterson

Edgar Allen Poe

Alexander Pope

John Wilmot, Earl of Rochester

Christina Rossetti

Sir Walter Scott

William Shakespeare

P. B. Shelley

Edmund Spenser

Algernon Swinburne

Alfred Lord Tennyson

Edward Thomas

Walt Whitman

Oscar Wilde

William Wordsworth

W. B. Yeats

Anthologies &Collections

Restoration and
Eighteenth-Century Verse

Nineteenth-Century Verse

Poetry of the First World War

Love Poems

The Metaphysical Poets

The Wordsworth Book of Sonnets

DISTRIBUTORS
for the Wordsworth Poetry Library

AUSTRALIA

Reed Editions
22 Salmon Street
Port Melbourne
Vic 3207
Australia
Tel: (03) 646 6716
Fax: (03) 646 6925

GREAT BRITAIN & IRELAND

Wordsworth Editions Ltd
Cumberland House
Crib Street
Ware
Hertfordshire SG12 9ET

PORTUGAL

International Publishing Services Ltd
Rua da Cruz da Carreira, 4B
1100 Lisboa
Tel: 01-570051
Fax: 01-3522066

SINGAPORE, MALAYSIA & BRUNEI

Paul & Elizabeth Book Services
  Pte Ltd
163 Tanglin Road No 03-15/16
Tanglin Mall
Singapore 1024
Tel: (65) 735-7308
Fax: (65) 735-9747

ITALY

Magis Books SRL
Via Raffaello 31/C
Zona Ind Mancasale
42100 Reggio Emilia
Tel: 0522-920999
Fax: 0522-920666

SOUTHERN AFRICA

Struik Book Distributors (Pty) Ltd
Graph Avenue
Montague Gardens
7441
P O Box 193
Maitland
7405
South Africa
Tel: (021) 551-5900
Fax: (021) 551-1124

USA, CANADA & MEXICO

Universal Sales & Marketing
230 Fifth Avenue
Suite 1212
New York, NY 10001 USA
Tel: 212-481-3500
Fax: 212-481-3534